Madeleine

The Shadow Investigation

Written by Peter Scharrenberg

April 2019

Madeleine: The Shadow Investigation

Colophon:

Author: Peter Scharrenberg
Translation: Inhouse
Coverdesign: YHMedia, The Netherlands
Publisher: YHMedia, The Netherlands
© 2019 Peter Scharrenberg - All rights reserved

ISBN: 978-1-7308-2270-4
NUR: 402

"It is important to keep in mind that it is not illegal to sustain the thesis according to which Madeleine McCann died in the apartment of Praia da Luz and that her body was concealed by her parents."

Judge Maria Emilia Melo e Castro
McCann v Amaral – Final Determinations Concerning Facts
21st January 2015

Note: it is not an established fact that Gerry and Kate McCann or any other persons named in this book are guilty of the disappearance of Madeleine. They are innocent until proven guilty in a court of law.

This book is a collection of facts sourced from the Portuguese police files, witness statements, expert opinions, the Leveson inquiry papers, interviews, videos, transcripts, newspaper articles and from other material in the public domain.

1. Introduction

More than six hundred weeks have passed since Madeleine McCann went missing and after all this time it is still not clear what really happened to her or where she can be found. That is the case if one believes the conclusions of the two police forces, namely the Polícia Judiciária and Scotland Yard, both of which are still investigating the mysterious disappearance in May 2007. It is hard to believe that they are still looking for a burglar; for after nearly twelve years both police forces should have realized that this line of enquiry is a dead end, but unfortunately, this is not the case. This deadlock can be deduced from the lack of public announcements regarding a breakthrough in the case and from the complete silence of those investigating this crime. It is highly likely that there is, nor has been a breakthrough at all, for otherwise the much criticized Scotland Yard detectives would have informed the public. They would probably have shouted it from the rooftops, for it would have silenced the critics who have followed their investigation for many years. Moreover, they could say they'd been right all along and it really was an opportunistic burglar who got away with Madeleine. However, this particular break in the case will never happen, not now, not ever. The reason for this definite statement is simple: there was no burglar in the parents' apartment and consequently Madeleine wasn't abducted by a burglar. Not even by a paedophile burglar, for heaven's sake! As I stated in my first book about this case, 'The Truth Is Out There', there are more than enough facts and indications to dismiss the burglar theory. The police should never have taken this theory seriously, because it was clear at a very early point in the investigation that the first statements given by the parents were not confirmed by the results of the initial forensic investigation. Apart from that, the statements given by Gerry and Kate were not supported by the known facts. In the above mentioned book I also revealed the names of two crucial witnesses who appear to have been ignored or perhaps forgotten, but who both, just one day after the disappearance, had given incriminating statements concerning Madeleine's father. From the many reactions I received on this subject it appears that a large number of 'Madeleine followers', both in the UK and the rest of the world, had also overlooked these crucial statements. Apparently in no other book about this case were these two important witnesses mentioned.

Soon after the publication of my first book it became clear to me that I had to follow up with another book, which should go into greater depth and details of the case. In particular I would assess a number of important statements, to establish whether they could stand the test of reality. For this reason I would need to engage technical experts in various disciplines in order to test the veracity of these witnesses. Apart from that I would also have to analyze the extensive databank of telephone traffic to see if that might lead me to Madeleine's possible burial place. Indeed, I believe, in fact I'm a hundred percent sure, that Madeleine is no longer alive. This is the point of view which is presented in this book. I could have chosen to take the viewpoint that the parents had nothing to do with the disappearance, but in that case the book would have had few pages; for just one word describes what evidence [or indications] I have found to prove that the parents played no part in Madeleine's disappearance. That word is 'nothing'. In fact all indications, statements from independent witnesses and the results of the Portuguese police investigation all point in one direction, namely the active involvement of the parents in the 'abduction'. Taking all this into account I cannot, how hard I try, think of a scenario which exonerates the parents, taking into consideration all the available evidence about the disappearance. On the contrary, I can defend my point of view with very solid arguments to prove that Gerry, Kate and the entire holiday group, the so-called Tapas 9, were fully aware of Madeleine's fate.

In this book I will reveal the location of the most likely spot where the remains of Madeleine may be found, based on the 'pings' of Gerry and Kate's mobile phones. I will also present some facts which as far as I know have never been discussed before. From these it will become abundantly clear that there must have been a conspiracy and that there were a number of 'third parties' involved who have never been named in the investigation.

A few chapters from my first book about the case, 'The Truth Is Out There' have been incorporated in this book. In fact it is best to read that book first, but to give 'new' readers a better overview of the investigation I decided, after due deliberation, to add these few chapters. It will also enable the 'new' readers to understand the 'bigger picture'.

If this wasn't such a serious case I would add that I wish you much pleasure with this book. Instead of that however, I hope this book will give you sufficient information and insights to enable you to form your own opinion about what happened to Madeleine.

Peter Scharrenberg.

2. HOW IT BEGAN

A British mother on holiday in a Portuguese village raises the alarm and calls for help when she panics because she can't find her three-year old daughter who shortly before had been asleep in her bed. That bed is now empty. A search starts immediately in and around the holiday flat, apartment 5A of the 'Ocean club Resort' in Praia da Luz, but she is not found. Her parents, Gerry and Kate McCann, are desperate. They know immediately what has happened: their daughter Madeleine has been abducted by a paedophile who has broken into the apartment. The British media give the news priority over all other matters. The largest possible headlines tell the public that a British toddler who was on holiday in Portugal has been taken from her bed by an abductor. Meanwhile the tabloids and TV stations have sent their best journalists to Luz in Portugal in order to report all developments. What follows is an enormous media circus which is to continue for months and which captures the imagination of the UK. Overwhelmed by the massive presence of the world press in the small holiday village, the police pull out all the stops. Extensive searches are initiated with massive numbers of officers called in, airports and harbours are kept under surveillance and road blocks set up. But Madeleine isn't found, and this is still the case, for twelve years later she is still missing.

A RECONSTRUCTION

It's about a 20.45h on the evening of the 3rd of May 2007 when Gerry and Kate McCann, both doctors, arrive at the Tapas bar which is part of the holiday complex where they are staying, to have dinner with their six friends, as has been their habit every evening of that holiday week. The Tapas bar is about a hundred metres walk from their holiday apartment where their three children, Madeleine, nearly four years old, and the twins, two years old, are all asleep. The parents take it in turns to go back to their apartment during the evening to check if the children are still sleeping and that everything is quiet. Gerry is the first to check the children that evening and sets off about 21.05h to do the first check on the apartment. When he turns the key in the front door lock he worries if the noise of the key turning will wake one of the children. He walks very softly to the children's room, takes two paces into the room and sees the twins lying in their travel cots and Madeleine in her bed. It's quiet, they are all asleep, so Gerry turns round and leaves the room. He uses the toilet and then walks back to the Tapas bar. Just outside the apartment he meets an acquaintance he has met during tennis lessons and he has a short conversation with him about a tennis tournament to be held in the holiday complex. That acquaintance is Jeremy Wilkins, a TV producer. At about 21.20h Gerry is back in the Tapas bar and joins his wife Kate and their six friends. The McCann's friends are David and Fiona Payne, both of them doctors, Russell O'Brien, another doctor, and Jane Tanner, media consultant, Matthew Oldfield, doctor, Rachel Oldfield-Mampilly, recruitment consultant, and Diana Webster, the mother of Fiona Payne, who is on holiday with her daughter and son-in-law and is present at the table in the Tapas bar that evening. [At a later date the British Press will invent the name 'Tapas 9' for the group].

Everybody is in a good mood, drinking wine, laughing and joking, the friends are having a good time. Around 21.30h Kate gets up, it is her turn to check on the children but before she leaves the table Russell O'Brien and Matthew Oldfield offer to check on Madeleine, Sean and Amelie by listening at the shutters of their bedroom. They have to pass the apartment anyway to check on their own children. Kate hesitates but after a few seconds she appears to be happy with the offer from the two friends and sits down again. Ten minutes later Matthew Oldfield is back in the Tapas bar and he tells Kate everything is quiet in the children's room of apartment 5A. Half an hour goes by and Kate walks quickly via the badly lit path to the apartment; via the stairs to the balcony at the back Kate slides open the patio door and goes to the children's room, where she is shocked to see that the bed in which Madeleine lay asleep is now empty. The twins are still in their cots and are sleeping deeply. She searches the apartment but she can't find Madeleine. Completely panicked and overwrought she runs back to the Tapas bar, shouting: "She's gone! They've taken her! Gerry, she's gone!" Everybody at the table, except for Diana Webster, jumps up and runs with Kate to the apartment. Gerry runs ahead of the group. The friends check all the cupboards and possible hiding places in the apartment, but failing to find the little girl, they continue the search outside. The areas close to the holiday flat are quickly searched but there is no trace of Madeleine. By now everybody is panicked: where can she be? The decision is taken to call the police; one of the friends goes to the reception to arrange for it to be done. Kate is by now totally distressed and asks several times for a priest. Meanwhile, as it later transpires, one of the Tapas friends phones the media in the UK to inform them of what Gerry himself says: his daughter is abducted, probably by a paedophile burglar. The police have not yet arrived at this point as they are only alerted at 22.41h and arrive about 23.00h.

When the GNR [Guarda Nacional Republicana, the Portuguese gendarmerie] arrive on the scene, Gerry and Kate have already reconstructed what has happened: a burglar has entered the apartment by opening the shutters of the window and has taken Madeleine from her bed and taken her away with him through another window, the sill of which is about one meter from the floor. The soldiers, for that is what the members of the GNR are, notice that the shutters are partly raised and that the window itself is partly open. Is this the route taken by the intruder? Both the uniformed men listen to the story as told by the parents' and take the first statements. After that Gerry and Kate go to their bedroom. They now have to wait for the Polícia Judiciária, in short PJ, the police force which is concerned with criminal affairs, who will be in charge of the case. When inspector Vitor Martins and his colleague, specialist João Barreiras arrive around 00.45h that night, they immediately walk to the bedroom where both parents are said to be. Standing on the threshold of the bedroom they observe, as they recount at a later date, a somewhat curious scene. Gerry and Kate are on their knees next to each other at the end of the bed and like praying Muslims bent forward, banging their hands on the bedcovers, after which they rise up and wave their arms in the air. They go through this openly demonstration of grief several times, all their movements synchronised whilst shouting meaningless and apparently helpless phrases which are supposed to express their despair and sorrow. However the officer notes that there are no tears.

When things have quietened down Inspector Martins takes both parents' statements. Kate, Madeleine's mother, is absolutely sure: Madeleine has been abducted, by a burglar. Gerry, the father knows even better, abducted by an intruder, to pass on to a paedophile network in Portugal. No doubt the policeman will have wondered how they'd arrived at those quick conclusions, but he carries on with his questions. How did the burglar get in? Was there a door or a window left open? No, that was definitely not the case, according to both parents. Everything was locked. According to them the intruder managed to lift the shutters from outside and had entered the apartment that way. Who else could have raised the shutters? In any case, not the parents, as they stated. And the window wasn't open earlier either so that too must have been done by the burglar. Martins writes down their statements and tells them he will contact them in the morning. Meanwhile his colleague has made a photo report of all the rooms of the apartment, including some objects he finds of interest. The first investigation is finished. After this all the police leave apartment 5A and leave the parents alone with their friends. Around 04.00h in the morning Gerry and Kate go to sleep in the Payne's apartment not knowing where their three-year old daughter is. [Apartment 5A is now a crime scene so they couldn't stay there.]

[As later was established Gerry and Kate did not physically search for their daughter after the first superficial search. The search dog team arrived at 02.00h on May 4th 2007. The search by the GNR and numerous volunteers went on all night. The parents however, took some time around midnight, to delete all calls from their mobiles before the PJ arrived.]

The next morning the Portuguese police begins immediately with a forensic investigation of the shutters and the open window. Apart from the normal forensic officers, specialists of the better equipped LPC Crime Scene Unit also arrive at apartment 5A. It appears that fate favours the investigators as they hear from the resort's service manager that the apartment of the McCanns was thoroughly cleaned on Wednesday 2nd May, only one day before the disappearance. Officers believe that because the apartment was cleaned the previous day any fingerprints found will be easy to identify and facilitate the investigation. This could be a breakthrough in the investigation and help trace the little girl. Gerry and Kate are both adamant that they haven't opened the window and that it must have been done by the abductor. A remarkable statement, for when the result of the forensic investigation is complete, it proves that the fingerprints of just one person are found on the window: those of Kate McCann. And that's not the full story. The CSI team has rock-solid evidence that it's impossible to open the shutters from outside. The mechanism which operates them is constructed in such a manner that it is physically impossible to open them from outside. Moreover, there are no traces of burglary or other damage and indications which would point to there having been a burglary of any kind. On the outside wall too, under the window where according to the parents the abductor had climbed out, not a single trace was found to confirm the parents' version of events. Consequently these first investigation results show the parents in a new light, for who else but they themselves could have raised the shutters? But why? By giving these impossible explanations about the way the intruder got in and out, they draw the PJ's attention. Apparently the couple realized this for they then propose a second scenario. They next declare with absolute certainty that the abductor entered via the patio door, which all of a sudden was no longer locked but could be opened from outside and that afterwards he had climbed out through the children's small bedroom window with Madeleine under his arm. Logical question: why didn't he exit through the same door, but instead chose a difficult climb through a small window? Probably because Kate realized she shouldn't admit that she had touched that window but instead 'opened it by accident', therefore it had to be maintained as the escape route in the second statement; it might have looked strange if not only the shutters but also the small window now suddenly hadn't been opened by the abductor. For the next question would be: who did open the windows and shutters and why? All this put the parents in a difficult position, in effect there would be nothing left of their theory of burglary and abduction by a paedophile intruder. But Gerry and Kate stuck to their second statement about what had happened or what had to have happened and the investigators of the PJ got nothing more from them. The parents have never given another explanation on the matter of why the shutters were opened and who might have done so. Similarly, no explanation for Kate's fingerprints on the open window has ever been given by the McCanns.

3. TAPAS 9

Professor Gerald Patrick McCann, the father of Madeleine, is born on the 5th of June 1968 in Glasgow, Scotland. He completed his study in medicine at the University of Glasgow in 1992. In 2000 he was appointed 'specialist registrar' in Cardiology at the University of Leicester. He completed his post-doctoral studies in 2011 and his Career Development Fellowship in 2014 after which he was awarded a research professorship at the University of Leicester. He is also co-chair of the BSCMR Cardiovascular Research group in the East Midlands and chairman of the MRI trust clinical research advisory group as well as being Chairman of the British Cardiovascular Society, a specialized clinical research group for illnesses related to aortic valves. At the time of the disappearance he was a consultant cardiologist and medical advisor for a sub-committee which advised the government on issues regarding the safety of various kinds of radiation [COMARE]. He is a good friend of Dr. David Payne, one of the Tapas 9.

Dr. Kate McCann-Healy is Madeleine's mother and she was born on the 5th of March 1968 in Liverpool, England. Kate studied medicine at the University of Dundee in Scotland. She specialized in gynaecology and later in anaesthesia. At the time of the disappearance Kate worked as a locum GP in Melton, Leicestershire. Kate married Gerry in 1998. Both Madeleine and the twins Sean and Amelie were conceived using IVF .

Dr. David Payne is married to Fiona. He was a Senior Fellow in cardiovascular sciences at the University of Leicester and worked until recently in the Leicester General Hospital. It is not known where David Payne works at present. His mother-in-law had joined the Paynes for their short holiday in Portugal. David and Fiona were the only couple who had a working baby monitor so that they wouldn't have to leave the table to check on the children.

Dr. Fiona Payne is also a very good friend of Gerry and Kate. She saw, according to her testimony, a suspicious person in the vicinity of the McCann apartment. This person was never traced. Fiona and her husband David stayed on in Praia da Luz to support Gerry and Kate and didn't leave for the UK until much later. It is Fiona who said about the Thursday afternoon the 3rd of May that 'the men were sort of out of the picture.'

Dr. Russell O'Brien completed his study in medicine at the University of Leicester in 1994 and worked as a consultant in Clinical Pharmacology and General Internal Medicine before he moved to Exeter. He is also the Director of the so-called BNBS Programme and Associate Director of clinical Studies at the Peninsula College of Medicine and Dentistry. Both in Exeter and at the Peninsula College he is the Head of the Academic Clinical Pharmacology. Jane Tanner was Russell O'Brien's partner at the time of the disappearance. They have two children. In 2011 Russell raised money via 'Force', a charity website which organized a 100 mile bike ride which collected donations for cancer treatment and for the McCanns.

Dr. Matthew Oldfield is married to Rachel and he worked at the time as an endocrinologist in Kingston Hospital in Surrey. [Endocrinology is the branch of physiology and medicine concerned with endocrine glands and hormones.] At a later date he worked with Gerry McCann in Leicester. Matthew and Rachel moved to London a little time later. It was Matthew who did the 'check' on the children of the McCanns that Thursday night about 21.30h. He was unable to see whether Madeleine was there because he didn't actually enter the children's room. He didn't see the raised shutter in the apartment and he also missed the wide open window through which the curtains blew in the wind.

Rachel Oldfield-Mampilly is married to Matthew Oldfield. She studied Law and worked at the time of the disappearance as a recruitment consultant for a firm in London. Rachel stated, as did Fiona, that she had seen a suspicious man near the apartment of the McCanns. She and Matthew have a daughter who at the time of the disappearance was about one-and a half years old.

Jane Tanner was the partner of Russell O'Brien with whom she has two children, a daughter about one-and a half years old and another daughter aged three at the time of the disappearance. At that time Jane Tanner worked as a marketing consultant. It was Jane who saw a man with a child in his arms on the evening of the disappearance. It was generally assumed that this was the actual abductor carrying Madeleine. The abduction theory was for the greatest part based on this statement. However, the Portuguese police discovered important discrepancies in Jane's testimony and therefore she was seen as an 'unreliable' witness. Jane maintains even now that she saw a man walking with a girl in his arms, very close to the McCann apartment.

Diana Webster is Fiona Payne's mother and she accompanied her daughter and son-in-law David to the Algarve where she stayed in the same apartment as the Paynes. Diana Webster could not give a decisive answer as to when she last saw Madeleine that week. She alone stayed at the table in the Tapas bar when the rest of the group hurried to the apartment of the McCanns. Diana Webster has always avoided the media after her return to the UK.

4. Jane Tanner, part 1

Jane Tanner, one of the Tapas 9 and partner of Dr. Russell O'Brien, is in the spotlight of the investigators the day after the disappearance when she tells the police that she is able to give a good description of the man with a child in his arms, the man she has seen near apartment 5A, at about or even exactly the time of the abduction. This surprising declaration hits the investigating team like a bomb. Naturally Jane Tanner is asked to contact the PJ immediately to tell them all she knows. Is this the break they're waiting for? Can Jane give a good description of the man so that they will be able to focus on the type of man the abductor was? Expectations are high when Jane arrives at the police station in Portimão.

The inspectors are not disappointed; witness Jane Tanner gives a detailed description of both the man and the child she saw around 21.15h that evening, very near to apartment 5A. She declares that the man was between thirty-five and forty years old, that he had dark hair down to his neck and was dressed in light-coloured trousers with a dark jacket or anorak. He was carrying a small blond girl wearing light-coloured pyjamas, probably white or pink, and the girl was barefoot. The officers are over the moon; they now have a lead to a possible abductor. Immediately a priority all-agency APB is sent out with the descriptions to all police stations, airports, seaports and border posts, with the request to look for the man, who would most probably have a blonde English-speaking toddler with him, possibly in white pyjamas and barefoot. The all points bulletin is the first logical action the PJ took after they've received such a detailed description of the abductor from Jane Tanner.

But the officers want to know more, in fact they want to know everything and Jane Tanner appears unprepared for such a detailed interrogation. It is possible that she thinks that by giving a description her task is done but in fact the real work is just beginning. What follows are hours of interviews where the smallest details are asked: 'Did she hear a car door slam? What colour was the light from the lamp post? What was the temperature? Did she hear a dog bark?' Jane seems to do the best she can during these interviews but has trouble remembering details which should be far easier for her to recall. Remarkably, one of her most important statements is not supported by two other important witnesses. Apart from that a number of details in her statement do not tally with the results of the PJ's own investigations, something that the interrogating officers can't fail to notice. For the first time since the interviews of all concerned have started, it is obvious to the officers in Portimão that there are serious differences in the statements. And after a thorough evaluation the investigators can only come to one conclusion: Jane Tanner isn't telling the truth; she has made false statements. The PJ therefore decide that she is an unreliable and totally incredible witness. And they can prove it too. Thanks to two of their sniffer dogs, about which more later. Why the investigating team come to this remarkable conclusion will be made clear in the account of the reconstruction, which starts on the evening of the disappearance of Madeleine, around 21.00h that night.

A RECONSTRUCTION

Jane Tanner, her partner Russell O'Brien and their friends are sitting around a large round table in the Tapas Bar where they dine every night. They have already ordered from the menu and are waiting for the starters to be served. Jane notices that Gerry McCann gets up to check Madeleine, Sean and Amelie. It's just after 21.00h. Jane wonders if she should go with him to listen at her window to see if all is well with her own children. But Gerry is already on his way and she decides to wait until she has finished her starter. But, around 21.30h Jane gets up, it's her turn to check her children and she walks over to the apartment complex. As she arrives there she sees Gerry. He is standing on the pavement talking with a man she only knows by name: Jeremy Wilkins. She passes them without acknowledging them and walks via a small crossing to her apartment, where all is quiet and peaceful, she then returns to the Tapas bar. On her way back she notices that Gerry and Jeremy are gone from the spot where she saw them five minutes earlier and she assumes that Gerry is back in the Tapas bar. Once back in the Tapas bar she sits down at the table, happy that her turn to check is complete. The starters are then served and the whole group tucks in. Around 21.30h Jane sees her partner Russell and Matthew Oldfield get up from the table. She notices they offer to do Kate's check on Madeleine, Sean and Amelie as well to see if all is quiet, so that Kate can stay at the table and skip her round of checks. Kate accepts the offer and the men walk towards the exit of the Tapas restaurant, on their way to do the checks at the apartment complex. Ten minutes later Jane notices that only Matthew Oldfield has returned from checking on the children. He tells her that Russell has stayed in their apartment as little Evie was awake and has been sick. Jane finishes her main course and has Russell's main course returned to the kitchen where it will be kept warm. Around 21.45h she gets up and tells the group that she is going to relieve Russell to give him the opportunity to finish his meal. Jane decides to stay in her apartment with her sick daughter for the rest of the evening. At about 22.10h Jane hears shouting outside the apartments. It appears to be Kate's voice, she is screaming that Madeleine has gone. Because Jane thinks she hasn't heard it properly she goes outside and sees to her surprise that all her holiday friends are running from the Tapas bar to the apartment complex, Gerry in front of the others. She had heard correctly: Kate screams that Madeleine is gone. She doesn't join the first searches, but stays with her daughter Evie, who is still awake. But as soon as the GNR arrives she tells them about a 'man with a child' she has seen earlier. Later that evening she also passes this information on to the officers of the PJ, who carefully note her statement. After this she returns to her apartment where she falls asleep around 03.30h. This concludes the reconstruction of the evening of the 3rd of May 2007, seen through the eyes of Jane Tanner.

As was noted earlier in this chapter: Jane Tanner is seen as an unreliable witness and her statements are regarded as incredible by the officers of the PJ. It seems they have more than enough reasons for their skepticism. They have serious reservations about her witness statement regarding the accidental meeting she states she had with Gerry and Jeremy Wilkins, when she was on her way to her apartment to check on her children. Both Gerry and Jeremy state during their interviews with the PJ that they didn't see Jane Tanner. They add that it is very unlikely, if not impossible, that they would not have noticed her, taking into account the narrow pavement of the street. The investigators find this strange. Why would Jane lie about this? In later interviews with the police both men stick to their earlier statements: they haven't seen Jane Tanner. Jane for her part, sticks to her guns; she has definitely seen both men. To keep things clear: Gerry and Jeremy, according to their statements, were definitely there around 21.15h, having a conversation.

Another thing the Portuguese investigators do not understand is that neither of the two men have seen the man with the child in his arms walking on the narrow crossing up the road. Considering the short distance between the spot where both men were standing and the crossing, no more than a few metres, this seems unlikely. The men also stick to their first statements: if somebody had crossed the road there then they would certainly have seen him. This situation is, to put it mildly, curious. How is it possible that three people, Jane, Gerry and Jeremy, who were in such close proximity to each other, didn't all see the same thing? And not even noticed each other? What further surprises the investigators is the sudden activity of both Russell O'Brien and Jane Tanner that evening of the disappearance. Between the two of them they were going to and from between the restaurant and the apartment because their daughter Evie was sick and could not sleep. A logical story, if your little girl is ill she can't be left alone. But that was exactly what the officers of the PJ were thinking: that is a really good excuse to be with your daughter and importantly, out of sight, because you had something else to do? This thought arose for the following reason: Dr. Russell O'Brien said in his official statement for the police that his daughter was ill and had been sick. He had cleaned her up and had put the bedding and her pyjamas in the washing machine. Possibly to make his story more believable Dr. O'Brien said that he'd phoned the service desk to ask for clean bedding to be brought to the apartment. When the PJ checked this statement it appeared that the service desk had not received such a telephone call. The investigating team was puzzled. Why would Dr. O'Brien say any such thing when it was apparently not true? Why would he do that? The officers couldn't think of a logical reason for this behaviour; apparently the pair O'Brien and Tanner, were being 'economical' with the truth. But why? Why are they making untrue statements? What's in it for them? When confronted with the statement from the service desk, Dr. O'Brien says nonchalantly that the service manager must have forgotten that he'd phoned them.

Back to Jane Tanner and her statement that when she was walking towards a narrow intersection at the top of the road, she saw a man with a small child in his arms crossing the road. This witness statement is not at all supported by two experienced police sniffer dogs, who repeatedly and independently of each other, followed Madeleine's scent from apartment 5A for some distance. But despite many attempts by the dog handlers they found no scent of Madeleine anywhere near the junction where Jane Tanner says she saw the man with the child, the theoretical abductor with Madeleine in his arms. However, the dogs took their handlers several times across another road, the Rua Dr. Francisco Gentill Martins, the 'abductor' would logically have taken with Madeleine, on the way to 'downtown' Praia da Luz. Gerry explained this by stating at a later date that the dogs could be right because he'd walked there the previous day with Madeleine. But in his earlier statement he said that neither he nor Kate had been outside the resort that day.

Another clear indication that Jane didn't see the man is evident when she describes how the man carried Madeleine. According to Jane she saw the legs and bare feet of the child when the man passed her sightline from left to right. This means that the man had the head of the girl on his left arm, whilst his right arm supported the legs of the child. At first glance this is an innocent remark from Jane. But this can't be right either. For there is a very good reason to suppose that the child could not have been carried in that way by the supposed abductor. It is necessary to look at the way the children's bedroom was arranged and in particular the position of Madeleine's bed. Her bed was on the left, along the wall opposite the window and the head against the side wall. This means that Madeleine could only have been lifted out of her bed from the right-hand side of the bed. So: standing on the right side of the bed the 'abductor' has to have lifted her up with both arms. His right arm underneath her head and his left arm under her legs. If he in fact held her like that when leaving the apartment, and why wouldn't he, this means without doubt that Jane should have seen the head of the child as the man passed her viewpoint and not the little legs. This is exactly the opposite of the description Jane has given. Of course it is possible that after the 'abductor' had left the apartment he turned Madeleine around in his arms, but considering the distance between the apartment and the spot at which Jane maintains she has seen the 'abductor', about fifteen metres, this appears unlikely. It is rather an indication that this is a scenario invented by Jane, not something experienced by her. And the difference between making something up or remembering something is very great. Therefore the conclusion reached by the PJ about the unbelievable and unreliable evidence submitted by Jane Tanner is fully justified. But even so, her statements are certainly significant.

5. THE SMITHS' STATEMENTS

The statements given to the Polícia Judiciária by the Smith family from Ireland can be seen as the most important statements in the files. Unfortunately they weren't taken seriously by the detectives of the PJ, which means that those statements have not been thoroughly investigated. But in fact the three members of the Smith family who gave these statements could be key witnesses in the case. As will become clear in other chapters in this book. [In 'The Truth Is Out There' the statements of the Smiths are examined in greater detail.] The Smith family were enjoying a short holiday in Praia da Luz where Martin Smith and his wife Mary own a holiday home. That week their son Peter and daughter Aoife were with them; also there were Peter's wife Sile and four small children. On the evening of Madeleine's disappearance they were all walking home, after a meal in the 'Dolphin' restaurant and a short visit to 'Kelly's bar', to their apartment on the Estrela da Luz complex. On their way there they meet a man coming the opposite way who passes them in a narrow street, his head a little bent forward. He is carrying a young blond girl on his arm. The girl appeared to be asleep and her feet were bare. The family glanced at the man and the child and talking amongst themselves they walked on towards their apartment. The time is about 21.45h, Thursday evening the 3rd of May 2007, the evening of the disappearance. It is some time later when Martin Smith, back in Ireland, takes note of the ongoing media storm around the disappearance and starts to think. When exactly did that little girl disappear? Was I still in Praia da Luz at the time? He read in the newspaper that she disappeared on Thursday the 3rd of May, in the evening around 21.15h. to be precise. He tries to remember that specific day. Suddenly Martin Smith remembers the meeting with the man with the sleeping girl on his arm. Which evening was that? He does remember the date when Peter flew back home, that was the 4th of May. So they must have met the man with the child on the 3rd of May? On the evening she disappeared? Martin Smith can't let go of the idea that he has seen something that's very important. Had that man something to do with the disappearance of that girl and is it even possible that he was the abductor? Martin Smith decides to consult those of his family who were with him that evening and find out if they too remembered that man. Which they did. So after a short family conference it was decided that he would contact the Portuguese authorities. Of course the police was very interested in what the Smiths had to say, so they asked if Martin, Peter and Aoife Smith would come to Portugal to give their statements. The PJ also asked the witnesses to keep this journey a secret, which they did. Once at the Portimão police station all three of the Smiths were able to give a good description of the girl and the man. And they all stated that it 'could very well be Madeleine' they saw on the arm of this man. After they had given their statements they flew back to Ireland, probably thinking that they had done their civic duty. A few months later, on the 9th of September, Martin Smith sees the return of the McCanns to England. When Gerry, with his son asleep on his arm came down the stairs of the plane, his head a little bent forward, Martin Smith had a 'flashback'. That was the man whom they encountered in Praia da Luz. The way he held his son in a rather unusual way, partly over his shoulder, triggered his memory; an 'action replay' as he later said. He was almost certain that it was Gerry he met that fateful evening. He was the man with the child! Martin Smith rings the police in Leicester. The policewoman who took the call wrote in her report that the witness Martin Smith was 'upset', and 'very worried' about what he had seen and that he'd been 'unable to sleep' since he'd seen the clip on BBC news on September 9. He gave a statement on the 20th of September and at a later date, on the 30th of January 2008, he gave an additional statement which was sent to the PJ and the Leicester Police. In this statement he said that he was up to 80% sure that it was Gerald McCann he saw that night. However, Martin Smith was unaware at the time that his and his family's earlier statements had been put aside as not relevant. For the investigators had decided that he could not have seen Gerry; it didn't fit the timeline they'd made. They concluded that it couldn't have been Gerry as he was in the Tapas restaurant at 21.45h, as all his friends had stated. This conclusion was also written in the final report when the case was shelved. How evidence to the contrary was overlooked by the PJ will become clear in a later chapter in this book. ['Forgotten Witnesses'] In any case, the statements of the Smith family are convincing; all four adult members, plus Aoife and the thirteen-year old boy in the group, saw 'the man with the child' and described him. [The other members of the Smiths group who didn't travel again to Portugal were interviewed in the UK.]

6. JANE TANNER, PART II

Jane Tanner's statements regarding the 'man with the child' and the fact that the PJ regarded her evidence as 'not credible' and she was therefore not a reliable witness, has far-reaching consequences which should have led to new insights in the disappearance. It is a little strange that an experienced group of officers and the public prosecutor did not look further than the usual themes explored by the police such as: is this person telling the truth and is it believable? Certainly important questions, but surely more questions should have been asked by the investigating team. Because why does she lie in her statements? For how can she describe situations where she was not present and can therefore not know what took place? Who told her in that case? And more such questions should have been asked. Unfortunately it appears that the investigating team never had a brainstorming session to find answers to these very interesting questions. Clearly, the priority was to find Madeleine but still, a large number of red flags should have come up once the decision was taken to set aside Jane Tanner's evidence as unreliable.

This is for the following reason: it is as certain as it can be that Jane Tanner has not seen the man with the child on the crossing she has pointed out to the police. Gerry and Jeremy's statements and the many searches by the two Portuguese sniffer dogs make that abundantly clear. It also seems certain that she never passed Gerry McCann and Jeremy Wilkins and has therefore not seen the two of them in conversation, standing on the narrow pavement in the narrow street. Both men said they had not seen her, but that was near impossible considering the street of a few metres across and the even narrower pavement.

More important than the question why doesn't she tell the truth, is the question how does she do it? How can she be a witness to actual events without having been there herself? She declares herself to be accurately informed about facts she cannot know first-hand, facts which someone else must have told her. For if she wasn't in that street at the time, how could she know that Gerry and Jeremy were there talking to each other? For both men have declared that they were there, having a short conversation. There is no other conclusion, somebody told her, and it is certainly not Jeremy who is one of the only two persons who know that this conversation took place. It is certain that Jane and Jeremy did not speak to each other that evening. Therefore the only possibility is that she has had this information at a much later time from Gerry McCann. All other possibilities are excluded. Gerry told her. How and where isn't important for the moment, but it appears almost certain that Gerry was the source of this information. But the most incriminating part of Jane's statements concerns her description of 'the man with the child', whom she could not have seen.

* Dark skinned individual, male sex, aged between thirty-five and forty, slim physical appearance, about 1.70m tall. Very dark, thick hair, longer at the back [she only managed to see him from the side]. He was wearing linen type cloth trousers, beige to golden in colour, a "duffy" type jacket [but not that thick.] His shoes were dark in colour, classic type. He had a hurried walk. He was carrying a child, who was lying on both his arms, in front of his chest. By the way he was dressed, he gave her the impression that he was not a tourist, because he was very 'warmly dressed'.

** About the child who appeared to be sleeping, she only saw her legs. The child appeared to be older than a baby. She was barefoot and was wearing what appeared to be cotton pyjamas of a light colour [possibly white or light pink]. She is not certain, but has the impression that a design was visible on the pyjamas, possibly a floral pattern. As regards these details, she did not know what Madeleine was wearing at the moment of her disappearance, because she did not talk to anyone about this. As concerns the man she saw, she only spoke to Gerald about this, not entering into details, and to the police.' (Jane Tanner witness statement 04 May 2007, 11.30h)

That she did not see the man and the child she describes is as certain as one can be from the facts. But all the same she gives practically the same description of the man as the four members of the Smith family who did actually see the man with the child. For the Smiths described the 'man with the child': thirty-five to forty years old, medium height and build, dark hair, short at the back, light trousers, dark jacket. Concerning the child in his arms they said: a little girl, apparently asleep, about four years old, dressed in white pyjamas with pink accents. Blonde, shoulder length hair and pale skinned. She was barefoot.

Jane's contradictory statement about the meeting with Gerry and Jeremy is in stark contrast with how closely her detailed description of the 'man and the child' resembles the statements of the Smith family. And that looks impossible. For if the 'man and the child' were in fact Gerry and Madeleine, it follows as night follows day, that Jane Tanner was aware not only of the events of the third of May 2007, but also knew what happened to Madeleine.

And that is not all. For both Fiona Payne and Rachel Oldfield said that Jane Tanner told them on the night of the disappearance that she saw a man with a child in his arms, close to apartment 5A. Is this a premeditated moment of misdirection? It does seem so. Another point to note is that Jane declared that she waited the whole night before she told Gerry about seeing the possible 'abductor'. Is that normal? Would one not let the worried parents know the moment you had the information? She also said that she didn't want to upset either Gerry or Kate more than they were already. But that can't be right either. For within a short time after Madeleine was found to be missing, Gerry and Russell O'Brien sat down at the table to draw up a timeline of the events and the checks on the children done that evening up to the time Madeleine was found missing. As an aide-memoire for later, they said. On this timeline is written amongst other points: '9.15h Jane sees man walking with child'. This means that her statement, which is that she'd waited a whole night before she mentions to Gerry and Kate what she has seen, cannot be believed. For according to the other statements Gerry was sitting at the table at the time when the timeline was written down. Is it possible that Gerry missed this? The first concrete indication that Madeleine was abducted? Wouldn't anybody at that table have said anything about that note? No one? Not even Gerry? Once again an incredible scenario, to which not a lot of thought was given.

There were in fact two timelines made by the group. When the officers of the PJ compared both, significant differences were found in the times noted. How emotionless the holiday group is becomes clear to the officers when they notice that both timelines are written on the ripped-off covers of Madeleine's colouring book. Wasn't there a single piece of paper around? A notebook or even a beer mat. How can you destroy a colouring book that belongs to your little girl who has just disappeared? Would you, if you were a mother, not want to keep everything that belongs to your daughter, because you're afraid that you'll never see her again, or even keep everything hoping for her return? The careless destruction of a colouring book of Madeleine, who at that moment has been missing for just a few hours, says a lot about the mentality within the holiday group: cold, business-like and heartless.

And Jane Tanner? She was interviewed again, about a year later in the UK. But she maintained that she had seen the 'man with the child' on the crossing which she had pointed out to the police at the time in Portugal. And with that last statement, the questionable role of Jane Tanner in the mystery of Madeleine's disappearance has [for the time being] ended.

7. THE TIMELINE THAT DOESN'T ADD UP

An important technique used by the police all over the world in criminal cases is the so-called 'timeline of events'. Everything with relevance to the case under investigation is listed, as are the names, times and locations where events took place according to the various witnesses. Such a timeline reveals discrepancies and similarities at a glance and makes it very clear where people were and at what time. Constructing such an overview is time-consuming work for all the information has to be integrated into one rational whole and it can be quite a puzzle to put it all together. But once constructed it gives, timewise, an excellent picture of the facts and the statements of those involved.

So it's not surprising that the PJ wanted to create such a timeline of the evening of the disappearance, in order to get an overall view of the 'positions' and activities of the entire Tapas group. As soon as this was done it became clear that there were a number of statements which were, to put it mildly, hard to explain. Although the timeline constructed by the PJ and how they applied it to the case was never published, but an analysis of the facts and the statements from the holiday group give an idea what that timeline looked like. Starting at 20.45h on the evening of Thursday 3rd May 2007, the timeline as set out below leaves no room for doubt: it doesn't add up.

So back to the situation as it was in the Tapas bar on the evening of Madeleine's disappearance. The timeline starts around 20.45h when the first members of the holiday group arrive in the restaurant. Around 21.00h the group is all there and they start dinner. Probably just after the starters Gerry McCann gets up from the table to do his children's check; he leaves the restaurant and walks to apartment 5A. By then it is about 21.10h. After his check, having assured himself that both the twins and Madeleine are fast asleep, he starts walking back towards the restaurant. But near the back entrance to his apartment he runs into tv-producer Jeremy Wilkins who is trying to get his 8-month old son to sleep by taking him for a walk in his pram.

Gerry has met him on the tennis courts of the resort and they have a short conversation on the street near apartment 5A. Gerry is back in the restaurant around 21.20h. According to all the members of the Tapas group Gerry didn't leave the table again until they were all alerted to Madeleine's disappearance. So that is Gerry's timeline.

Next comes the timeline of Jane Tanner, another member of the Tapas group and the partner of Russell O'Brien. According to her timeline that evening she left, at least according to her own statement, just a little later than Gerry in order to do her own children's check. This would be around 21.12h, which means that she would have arrived at the apartment building at the latest around 21.14h. This time would be backed up by the fact that Jane said that she saw Gerry talking to Jeremy, close to the back entrance to apartment 5A. She passed them without greeting them and walked on to her own apartment. After she had done her check she walked back to the restaurant and passing the back entrance to apartment 5A she noticed that Gerry and Jeremy had apparently ended their conversation and were no longer there. And that fits nicely, at least it backs up the other statements; Gerry was back in the Tapas bar by about 21.20h. But this is not all Jane saw when she walked to her apartment. As stated before, she saw Gerry and Jeremy. But at very nearly the same time, at some distance beyond the spot where the two men were talking, she saw somebody who drew her attention. It was a man carrying a small girl in his arms. The girl seemed to be wearing a pyjama and her feet were bare, as Jane noticed and said in her statement later. Although she only saw the man for a few moments, at some distance and in the dark, she managed to give a detailed description of him. So detailed that she even added certain minor details about the shoes of the man. A short time after Madeleine's disappearance has been discovered Jane makes a connection with the man she saw crossing the road when she was on her way to do her check. According to Jane this must have been the abductor carrying Madeleine in his arms. A theory which is accepted incredibly quickly by the entire Tapas group as the one and only truth. Not only by the holiday group but as will be seen later, also by the inspectors of the Polícia Judiciária in Portugal and as becomes clear at a later date, also by the detectives of Scotland Yard.

But back to where we left Gerry, back in the Tapas bar at 21.20h, Jane returns some two minutes later, about 21.22h. So the entire group is now seated around their table. But not for very long for about 21.30h Kate gets up. According to her own statement she says that she felt it was time to do another check on the children. At the same moment Matthew Oldfield gets up too, at least according to the statements, to do his own 'check'. He notices that Kate is also about to do her check and kindly offers to do it for her in her apartment. So she can relax and stay in the restaurant. Kate accepts his offer and sits down again. At that moment Russell O'Brien apparently feels it's about time for him to check on his children, so he too gets up. Together with Matthew Oldfield he leaves the restaurant. By that time it is about 21.32h. A few minutes later, about 21.37h Matthew returns to the restaurant and tells Kate 'all is quiet' in her apartment. He also tells Jane Tanner that Russell has stayed behind in their apartment because one of their children was ill and had been sick. This caused Jane to finish her main course more quickly than normal and directly after that she goes to her apartment to relieve Russell, so that he will have time to eat his dinner. By then it is about 21.45h. Shortly after this Russell returns to the restaurant and eats his somewhat delayed main course. Meanwhile it is about 22.04h and Kate decides that it's high time to check on the children herself. So Kate gets up from the table and leaves the restaurant. Around 22.10h she runs back into the restaurant screaming that Madeleine is missing. Immediately the entire group, apart from Mrs. Webster, leaves the Tapas bar and hurries to the apartment.

All the above is in the timeline which the PJ must have constructed. An overview of names, times and activities all laid out in order. At first it all sounds very normal and nothing in particular stands out. But appearances can be deceptive, as will become undeniably clear. The following is said to have happened: Gerry and Kate stated that an abductor had taken Madeleine, having entered the apartment by pulling up the metal shutters of the living room window and opening the sliding window of the children's room to climb out the apartment. [With Madeleine under his arm?] How does that fit into the timeline of that evening? Once again: Gerry runs into Jeremy Wilkins after his check on the children, the time is about 21.15h. Jane Tanner passes them, without speaking to them and at the same time sees a man who carries a small child wearing pyjamas in his arms. This man is later understood to be the abductor. Jane goes to her apartment and then back to the restaurant. Next we have Matthew and Russell getting up to check on their children. By then it is just over 21.30h. Russell goes directly to his own apartment and Matthew checks the McCann children on his own. He enters the apartment and goes to the children's room. But he doesn't enter the room and stands in the door opening from where he cannot see Madeleine's bed, but only Sean's and Amelie's cots in the middle of the room. Because everything is quiet he goes back to the door and leaves the apartment. 'All is quiet' he reports to Kate. And that could be the end of it, but it is not. Because that story just doesn't add up, in fact it is a quite impossible story. And here is why. If Jane has seen the abductor as early as 21.14h, than logically he has already been in the apartment. This means that the rolled-up shutters and the opened window would have been visible. Especially the open window and the white fluttering curtains would stand out. Is it possible that Jane, Russell and Matthew all missed that when they walked past the McCann apartment, as they have stated? The McCann apartment was on the ground floor so it was in their view. The story is even stranger when one considers that Matthew Oldfield, who after all was inside the apartment, didn't see that the window was open and that the curtains moved in the wind. He stood in the door opening and that is right opposite the opened window, just a few metres across from him. Neither did he see that the shutters were halfway up, so that there was more light in the room. Surely it is completely unbelievable that he missed all that. Why didn't he notice any of this? The answer is quite simple. He, Jane en Russell didn't notice anything because that specific situation didn't exist at the time they passed the McCann apartment. Which they didn't do just once, but twice, on the way there and the way back. No rolled up shutter, no open window, no fluttering curtains. They'd seen absolutely nothing out of the way for the simple reason that there was nothing of that sort to see at that moment. And it seems clear that they did not come up with this beforehand or realize that it was a logical consequence of the burglar-abductor story. Meaning that the shutters and the windows must have been open when they passed apartment 5A. This is a classic example of amateurs who get mixed up in criminal enterprises. Nothing quite fits and it becomes a story which needs to be adjusted all the time. From the above, we can conclude that in fact the first person who notices the rolled-up shutters, the open window and the fluttering curtains is Kate...

Adding extra weight to the fact that the shutters and window weren't open before 22.00h is the statement from an independent Portuguese witness who drove past the apartment at exactly that time, and looked at part of the apartment block without seeing anything unusual. No open window, no fluttering curtains. And those would have been very visible to anyone who passed that spot at 22.00h. So if the window was still shut when she drove by and apparently the abductor didn't open it, who did? And why? The only person who entered apartment 5A after 22.00h was Kate herself.

Considering all the above, is it unreasonable to say that Kate is the one who raised the shutters and opened the window? Can it be otherwise? Knowing that it was irrefutably established that the shutters were raised from inside the apartment, it being utterly impossible to do so from the outside. These facts, all of which the PJ must undoubtedly have considered, mean the burglar-abductor theory should have been dumped in the trash can and the parents should have been subjected to a strict interview by the Polícia Judiciária. All the above shows what can be discovered from even a short timeline of events. It is a marvellous instrument to clarify confusing situations. It surely looks like the McCanns have done their best to keep everything as confusing as possible, in order to derail the investigation. As Gerry said at a later date concerning the many reports, statements and speculations in the media: "One good thing to come out of all of this is that there is so much in the press, nobody knows what is true and what isn't." And that is still, even after twelve years, a very strange remark.

8. 'FORGOTTEN' WITNESSES

The morning after the disappearance the 'Ocean Club' resort was flooded with investigators of the PJ, whose main task was to ask literally everybody in the resort whether they had seen something 'suspicious' or had seen someone behaving in an unusual manner? The least indication of anything out of the ordinary could be important, as the police investigators knew all too well, therefore everyone connected to the 'Club' was interviewed. This included the many suppliers of the resort, the garbage collectors, the cleaners, the maintenance staff and so on. All of these were sought out by the police to make a statement. The residents of the nearby apartment buildings were also visited by the police; the detectives wanted to interview everyone. Naturally the staff of the Tapas bar who had been on duty that Thursday evening were interviewed; had they noticed anything unusual? Surely one might expect that somebody must have seen something. But the diligent police officers didn't get lucky. By midday they still hadn't found a single clue which could further their investigation; apparently no-one had seen anything that could possibly have anything to do with the disappearance. Okay, there was one statement concerning a somewhat suspect person, a 'Rasta', but this information came from just one person and could not be corroborated by any other witness. The police left it there, mainly because he had not been seen on the Thursday evening by this one witness. It was beginning to look the detectives would have to go back to headquarters in Portimão without any useful information. All that remained to be done was to interview the staff of the Tapas bar, in particular those who had been on duty the previous evening, although the police officers didn't expect much in the way of useful information. After all, the 'kidnap' hadn't happened in the restaurant. But perhaps somebody had noticed something in the days before the disappearance, but thinking 'nothing ventured, nothing gained', they continued the interviews. Armed with their notebooks the investigators asked the Tapas bar restaurant staff one after the other to take a seat at their table. But once again, nobody had seen anything out of the ordinary, either on the day of the disappearance or on the days preceding it. The hard-working police still didn't get any useful information. But that was about to change. For when one of the kitchen staff, Svetlana Vitorino, of Russian descent, takes her place at the table to answer their questions, she states something remarkable. Below is part of her statement as it was written down by the officers at that time. [Statement Friday May 4 2007, the first day after the disappearance.]

Svetlana Starikova Vitorino _[Russian citizen, telephone No9663 5###],_ _kitchen assistant._
—Said that, yesterday, one individual, <u>supposedly the father of the missing, left the</u> _<u>dinner table</u> where a group of friends [in number 8 or 9] [....] <u>for about 30</u>_ _<u>minutes</u>. After having returned<u>, a woman who she believed to be his wife</u>, also left_ _the table, there having passed a few moments, all the guests left the table in_ _question, except one elderly lady, who told her [Svetlana's] colleagues that that_ _child had disappeared._

We already know that Kate left the Tapas bar around 22.00h to check on her children and that she came back in the restaurant about 10 minutes later, screaming that 'she' was gone. So in fact this witness said that Gerry wasn't present in the restaurant between 21.30h and 22.00h. For according to this witness, Gerry had only just returned before Kate left the restaurant. Unfortunately the police investigators didn't realize at the time how significant her statement was and therefore they didn't ask her for further details. One can't really blame the officers, for they already knew that members of the holiday group would get up from the table to see if their children were sleeping peacefully. They probably thought it was part of the usual behaviour pattern of the group. But this is not all. Because when Svetlana Vitorino gets up and the next witness sits down at the table, the investigators actually get confirmation of her statement. For it is Joaquim Baptista, a waiter from the Tapas restaurant, who has taken

Svetlana's place. Just like her, he was on duty on the evening of the disappearance and he too has noticed something. This is what he told the police.

[Statement Friday May 4 2007, the first day after the disappearance.]

__Joaquim Jose Moreira Baptista__ [residing at Rue Ilha Terceira, no##, in Lagos. Telephone No 91277####], table employee [waiter].
- Of the group of 8/9 British citizens who dined at the restaurant last night, as usual, of which the parents of missing were part [he didn't know them] he noticed that two individuals left the table, of the male gender. The first to leave was about 40/45 years old [tall, skinny white complexion, with large [a full head of] hair of colour gray] and the period of his absence was about 15 minutes, being that they had to [re-]heat his food, which had cooled.
__The second to leave__ [about 40/45 years of age, having the physical characteristics of the first, but having less bulky hair] did __so for about 30 minutes__, and that shortly after he returned, all left the table, except for an elderly person, who told him that a child had disappeared, the daughter of a member of the group, due to which he thought __that the second person to leave could have been the father of the child.__

As appears to be clear from this statement, he too saw Gerry get up from the table and leave the restaurant. And he too estimated that Gerry had been absent from the table for about 30 minutes. Just like his colleague Svetlana Vitorino he sees a connection between Gerry's return in the restaurant and the moment that a 'panicked' Kate came back to the restaurant. In fact this means that Joaquim Baptista stated that Gerry wasn't in the Tapas restaurant between 21.30h and 22.00h. It becomes clear that the witness statements of Vitorino and Baptista agreed on every point concerning Gerry's absence in the restaurant. Unfortunately it escaped the attention of the investigators.

Although witness Baptista says in his statement that the second person to leave the table '*could have been*' the father of the child, the chance that he was mistaken is in fact zero. For three days later he says in a following statement, made at the police headquarters in

Portimão, that *'he clearly recalls the appearance of the girl's parents'* [who entered the restaurant that evening]. As is quoted below.
[Statement Saturday May 6 2007, the third day after the disappearance]

Joaquim Jose Moreira Baptista:
- When asked he says that he clearly recalls the appearance of the girl's parents, he does not know their names, together with a group of English tourists who generally accompanied them, as for almost a week prior to the disappearance they would dine practically every day in the Tapas restaurant.

It is clear that the statements of these two witnesses are crucially important. For on the evening of the disappearance they place Gerry outside the restaurant in the same time frame: between 21.30h to 22.00h; independently of each other witness Vitorino and witness Baptista both have observed the same events, there cannot be any doubt about this whatsoever. The investigators however are unaware of the fact that they have just recorded two very important statements. For these statements open up the possibility of exploring scenarios other than an abduction, to discover what has happened to Madeleine. It isn't surprising that the PJ didn't immediately understand the importance of these two statements. It was the first day after Madeleine went missing, a definite timeline had not yet been constructed, but they already knew that the parents would leave the table from time to time to check on their children in the apartments to see whether all was quiet. On the basis of these facts the statements of the Tapas staff were not exceptional.

After a few days, once all the members of the holiday group have given their statements, it becomes clear that the statements of Vitorino and Baptista do not agree with those of the holiday friends. They all said that Gerry was in the restaurant between 21.30h and 22.00h. And because there was no reason at that time to find the discrepancy suspicious, it appears that these two witness statements were completely forgotten. However, on the 27th of May 2007 this situation should have changed immediately when the Smith family from Ireland told the PJ they had met a 'man with a child' in Praia da Luz around 21.45h. That was the moment when these two statements should have been revisited, all of a sudden here was the possibility that Gerry had not been in the Tapas bar, simply because he had been seen in another location at that particular time. 'Forgetting' the two witnesses from the Tapas bar closed an avenue of investigation concerning Gerry's presence there. Which is why, as has now become clear, it's totally unjustified that Gerry's presence in the Tapas bar has never been in doubt. The two statements of the Tapas bar employees added to the four statements of the Smith family should have led to an immediate and intensive investigation into Gerry's activities that evening. However, this didn't happen. And that is a pity as the solution of the mysterious disappearance seems to come closer if the witness statements of the Tapas bar employees and the Smith family are believed to be true. Because suddenly most pieces of the puzzle fall into place, creating an almost complete picture of what happened and what múst have happened to Madeleine.

Whichever way one looks at it; it is unbelievable that the PJ completely failed to understand the importance of the two crucial witnesses Vitorino and Baptista. It is quite likely that the cause is an administrative error. Because the important statements of these witnesses were given in the resort and were noted down by the investigator in his notebook. All witnesses who had been interviewed on the first day after the disappearance were told that they needed to present themselves at the police station in order to make an official statement which they had to sign. The statements which the investigator had written down in the resort were not signed by the witnesses. But in the statements signed at the police station there is no mention at all regarding Gerry's absence from the table on Thursday evening. Could it be that the police officer had forgotten to add their hand-written 'resort statements' to the official files? And that possibly these weren't added until much later? It would explain why the police investigators never bothered to interview these two important witnesses again or to re-evaluate their statements. And that is not only a serious blunder, but more than anything else a missed opportunity to discover the true course of events of that evening in Praia da Luz.

9. Serious errors

The official final report of the Portuguese police which was sent to the Attorney General and contained the results of the investigation, completed on the 14th June 2008 and published on the 4th August 2008, contains a very serious error. So serious in fact that this may well be called a crucial error which for eight years may have derailed the British investigation. Inspector João Carlos, who was responsible for Volume 17 of the final report, pages 4592 to 4649, submitted his written 'conclusão' on the 24th June 2008 and signed it off. However, the report has a demonstrable mistake. A crucial mistake in fact. One which has far-reaching consequences for this means that the important and revealing statements by four key witnesses played no role in the investigation. This same mistake appears in all known translations of this report, including that of the official translation from Portuguese to English. The Departamento De Investigação Criminal de Portimão, under whose aegis the Polícia Judiciária investigated the disappearance, falls under the responsibility of the Ministério da Justiça in Lisbon. But there too, the mistake doesn't seem to have been discovered. The part of the final report containing the glaring mistake:

'Martin Smith was questioned, who said that at the beginning of the Travessa da Escola Primaria he saw an individual carrying a child, walking in the opposite direction, at a normal pace, when he passed this individual it must have been about 22.00, being totally unaware that a child had disappeared.

'This witness was heard again by the Drogheda Irish police on June 23 2008 having been shown a video clip of Gerald McCann's departure by plane carrying one of the twins. This witness maintains his belief that judging by the posture, there seemed to be a probability of 60-80% that the person seen by him at about 21.55h at the previously mentioned place, was Madeleine's father. At this time, Gerald's presence at the restaurant was confirmed by his friends and has not been denied by restaurant employees'.

This last sentence is actually incorrect. Right there it all goes wrong, seriously so. For the fact is, as we now know, that there definitely were [two] restaurant employees who had contradicted the above statement and told the police that Madeleine's father was absent from the table in the restaurant for a longish period of time. It is impossible to understand how a mistake of this magnitude was made by the Portuguese investigation team. Not only that, it is a mistake with far-reaching consequences because it eliminated the statements from the Smith family from the enquiry, resulting in the fact that Gerry McCann was never considered to have been 'the man with the child'. Could that have been the reason that Scotland Yard, partly or wholly because of this fact, or only because of this fact, made it known right at the start of the British investigation ['Operation Grange' in 2011], that Gerry and Kate McCann were not, and would not be seen as suspects, as they were not considered to have been involved in the disappearance of their daughter? For it was set in concrete so to speak, that Gerry was in the restaurant at that time. But as one can see from the above fact, this is not at all certain.

Consequently we now have a new direction to follow: thoroughly investigating the statement of these possible key witnesses. For the first time in twelve years we can publicly cast doubt on the statements given to the police regarding the presence of Gerry in the restaurant the evening of Madeleine's disappearance. For years the 'fact' that Madeleine's father was present at the table in the Tapas restaurant during this crucial period that evening, has gone unchallenged. But this 'fact' was only based on statements given to the police by Gerry and Kate themselves and those of their holiday friends. However, the above mentioned witnesses placed Gerry outside the restaurant in the very same period that Madeleine disappeared. Who is right and who has been 'mistaken'? One might expect at the very least that the important witnesses Baptista and Vitorino would be named in the official final report of the Portuguese police, but for some reason this wasn't done and the question is why not? Had the PJ completely forgotten about these statements or didn't they even know they existed? The mistake discussed above is not the only problem. There is yet another mistake, a serious mistranslation in the English version of the final Portuguese report. As it happens in a statement which is one of the most important ones in the files.

According to the English translation the Russian-born Svetlana Vitorino [one of the two 'forgotten' witnesses] said in her statement to the investigators that she did not see 'purportedly' the father of the abducted girl in the restaurant between 21.30h and 22.00h. Purportedly? That isn't very strong. As an example of the correct use of the word 'purportedly': purportedly he is rich, but in fact he's poor. Purportedly is used to convey that you are wrong, that you didn't see it right. No, 'purportedly' is a weak term.

The question is: would a Russian woman who works in Portugal even know the Portuguese word 'purportedly' and also know how to use it correctly? The Portuguese word for 'purportedly' is 'aparentemente'. However, after reading the original PJ files, which are of course written in Portuguese, it becomes clear that not the word 'aparentemente' is used by her, but the word 'supostamente'. The English translation for this word is not 'purportedly' but 'supposedly'. And that's a big difference. The word 'supposedly' is much stronger than 'purportedly', which changes the validity of the statement and gives it a far more positive meaning. So now her statement reads: 'I suppose the father of the girl...'. That is quite different to the mistranslated 'purportedly'.

How this mistake could have been made in the translation without it being noticed is a mystery. The consequence of all this however is that the investigating officers of Scotland Yard read the statement, if they did so at all, and found it rather too vague, whilst in reality this is not the case. In this new correct translation she actually told the PJ that a person she 'supposes' to be Madeleine's father, had not been present in the Tapas restaurant for a good half hour. That it is just in this important statement where the mistake was made makes one think. Especially since it is now certain that this possibly crucial witness isn't even named in the official Portuguese final report. What matters is that a serious mistake was made in the translation of a witness statement, which changed the meaning of a crucial sentence. And that too may be called a very serious mistake.

10. Tuesday evening

When the group of friends are finally seated at the table in the Tapas bar that Tuesday night, it is evident that one member of the group isn't present: Russell O'Brien. He has stayed in his apartment because his little daughter Ella is ill; consequently he will not appear in the Tapas bar that evening. The Tapas 9 have become the Tapas 8 but as will become clear later that evening it will be the Tapas 7.

So what was going on Tuesday night? To start off with it was just the same as Sunday and Monday night: the entire group gathered in the Tapas bar waiting for their table, to have their evening meal together, amongst other things exchanging their experiences and stories of that day. Naturally whilst enjoying a relaxing glass of wine. The waiters would quickly lay the table for them after which drinks and starters were ordered which didn't take long to arrive to still the hunger and thirst of the holidaymakers. Nothing out of the way up to now. Furthermore, as is clear from the statements made later by the Tapas 8, nothing unusual happens apart from a quiz which had been organized for that evening. However, something does happen or must have happened, for Kate gets up from the table and leaves the restaurant.

The exact time this happened isn't known but it must have been before 21.30h and just after the main course was served. For around that time aerobics instructor Najoua Chekaya enters the stage so to speak. Gerry invites her to join him at the table, just for a pleasant chat. Some statements indicate that Gerry was rather charmed by the young aerobics teacher and it even looked as if he was openly flirting with her. But by then Kate had already left the table and wasn't in the restaurant. It is a reasonable assumption that Gerry would not behave like this in the presence of his wife, right in front of their holiday friends. Surely not? But this is not the most important reason to believe that Kate was no longer present in the restaurant by 21.30h. No, the most important reason is that the aerobics instructor says in her statement that she can't remember whether she saw Kate at the table when she sat down there. She did see the other members of the group, but not Kate. Furthermore, according to her statement, she saw an empty chair and an empty plate on the table. It was generally assumed that this empty plate was meant for Russell, but this is very probably not the case. For could it be Russell's empty plate? Was it actually meant for him? No, again that isn't likely, rather it is very unlikely. Why? Because the waiters would lay the table correctly and would immediately take away any superfluous settings and [wine]glasses. Seven guests are seven plates, seven wine glasses and seven sets of cutlery on the table and not either eight or nine complete place settings. This is how things are done in most well-run restaurants in the world, so one may assume that this was also the case in the Tapas bar in Praia da Luz that Tuesday night. It then follows that the empty plate wasn't Russell O'Brien's, for when the group entered the restaurant it was clear that Jane Tanner had come alone and therefore there was never a place set for Russell. So that empty plate could not have been his. However, the aerobics instructor is adamant: she did see an empty plate on the table an not only that, the chair in front of it was unoccupied, nobody was seated in front of the empty plate. However, the plate was on the table because somebody was seated there at the start of the meal and had probably consumed both a starter and the main course, without the sweet course. Someone other than Russell must have sat there otherwise the waiters would have removed that plate.

So, we have an empty plate, an unoccupied chair and a witness who didn't see Kate at the table when she was seated there herself. It seems very likely that Kate got up from the table before 21.30h and left the Tapas bar. It's interesting to consider what Kate could have done after that and where she was going. She left the restaurant, at least we presume she did. It was already dark around 21.30h and it wasn't really warm outside, in fact it was a bit chilly. As we learn later from one of her statements she felt uneasy when she had to do a children's check and had to cross to the apartment through unlit parts of the resort. So the chance that Kate would have felt like a brisk walk that evening isn't the first thing that comes to mind. But what else? What opportunities did Kate have? Of course she could just go straight to apartment 5A, but she didn't do that. For otherwise she would have said so in her statements, for instance that she was too tired, had a splitting headache or something similar. But nothing like that was said, apparently it was important for Kate to keep quiet about the fact that she had left the table early.

So she didn't go to her apartment, otherwise she would have said so. What else could Kate have done? Where could she in all likelihood have gone? There is really only one possibility: Kate has gone to see Russell; he was babysitting on his own in his apartment and of course Kate was well aware of that fact. Surely that is a realistic assumption? For where else could she logically have gone? Perhaps she had important matters to discuss with Russell O'Brien? But this is only Tuesday night, two days before Madeleine disappeared. What needed to be discussed at that time that had to stay secret?

Assuming that Kate has gone to see Russell and has stayed there for some time isn't the only unusual event. For suddenly Kate starts to send sms messages, the first one around 22.15h and the last one by 22.27h, six sms messages in total, in just about twelve minutes. The content of these has never been divulged, but it is generally assumed that Kate was in apartment 5A at that time. This is partly corroborated by the statements from the Tapas group that they never took their mobile phones with them to the restaurant. And it was also the first time that Kate used her mobile after dinner that week. So when Kate sends off the last sms at 22.27h she leaves her apartment and very probably returns to Russell's apartment. This can be argued as follows: when Kate sends off her last sms a few minutes pass before one of her children starts to cry. This begins around 22.30h according to Mrs. Pamela Fenn, a British neighbour who has a flat above the McCann apartment. Mrs. Fenn is very definite about what she heard, when she heard it and also the time when at which this took place. She stated that she was worried because she heard a child crying from 22.30h to 23.45h that Tuesday night. She added that the crying finally stopped when the parents came home at 23.45h. The McCanns have always maintained that the statement given by Mrs. Fenn was untrue. They say Mrs. Fenn is mistaken in the day; one of the children had cried on the Wednesday evening, not on Tuesday evening. But Mrs. Fenn, who has since passed away, was adamant that she was right. In any case she had called her friend Edna Glyn that Tuesday evening and had told her about the ceaseless crying. Mrs. Fenn insisted it was definitely on Tuesday evening.

What stands out here is that the McCanns made such a big deal out of this statement from the British upstairs neighbour. [It was this same neighbour to whom Gerry said 'there was a girl missing' when she asked him what was going on. A girl? Excuse me? His own daughter! Noteworthy: Gerry didn't bother to ask this upstairs neighbour immediately whether she'd perhaps heard or seen something suspicious that evening.]

Considering the detailed statement from Mrs. Fenn and the reference point she had by having phoned her friend, it does appear to be certain that the crying episode took place on Tuesday night. Consequently the only conclusion that can be reached is that Kate was no longer in the apartment when the crying began. That is taking into consideration that no parent will let a child cry for one hour and fifteen minutes, apart from the fact that listening to it would drive most parents mad. No, it seems reasonable to say that Kate had already left the apartment, otherwise the crying would have stopped earlier or would not even have started. She went out, most likely back to Russell, for where else could she go? What she did there is not known. What does become clear is that Gerry must have ended up there as well that evening, for he came back to apartment 5A together with Kate at 23.45h. It is also certain that Gerry and the other members of the group left the Tapas bar at the latest at 23.00h. Even so, Gerry didn't get back to his own apartment until 23.45h. In any case there is a 'gap' of 45 minutes that evening during which time the activities of the McCanns, or where they have been, is not known. But whatever they did do, it had to remain a secret, that at least is clear. Now it also becomes clear why the statement of Mrs. Fenn was discredited by the McCanns. For they insisted that the crying episode took place on Wednesday evening, for that time they were late coming back because, unlike any other evening, they had stayed in the bar to have a cocktail. But on Tuesday evening, according to the parents, they were back in the apartment 'at the usual time' and none of the children had cried.

But the McCanns were stuck with Mrs. Fenn's statement and for a very good reason. For her statement suggests that they were not in their apartment on Tuesday evening and that contradicted their own statements. They insisted that their presence with the children in the apartment at 23.00h would be be accepted. But this doesn't appear to be true, if only because the McCanns were so very keen to make everyone believe it was the truth, but the statement of Mrs. Fenn is set in stone. It seems clear that the activities of Kate and later also those of Gerry could not become known to others. For if that 'secret' meeting with Russell, Jane, Gerry and Kate [and perhaps even the entire Tapas group] did indeed take place, and it certainly looks like it, then the question arises what may have been discussed that evening until about 23.45h. And why should such a meeting be a secret? Was it necessary to hide something? Already that Tuesday evening? The statements of both Miss Najoua Chekaya and Mrs. Fenn are very important, most of all because they are very clear and precise and leave no room for doubt. Najoua Chekaya can't remember whether she has seen Kate at the table, but what she does remember is that there was an empty chair and an empty plate on the table. She had the impression that somebody had been seated there and had left. Mrs Fenn heard a child crying on Tuesday evening from 22.30h to 23.45h. Discussing this further is pointless. Mrs. Fenn wasn't stupid and she knew perfectly well which day she heard a child cry for one hour and fifteen minutes. Unfortunately the PJ has never paid attention to either of these two statements, but they are definitely significant. Because again, there are two witnesses who, independent of each other, have given important statements which apparently fit together perfectly. The question arises as to who is right and who has made a mistake. Mrs. Fenn was adamant, it was Tuesday evening. She could also recall exactly what she had done on Monday evening and also what she did on the Wednesday evening, the day following the crying episode, so her statement is certainly credible. Even concerning the time she said it happened, she had just been watching the BBC Ten O'Clock News, and could thus give an exact time when the crying started. Mrs. Pamela Fenn, may she rest in peace, gave an important statement regarding that Tuesday evening and this statement should have been taken seriously and investigated further. Typically, as happened often in this case, it was just these kind of statements which were disregarded by the Portuguese police. It didn't fit in the 'burglars story' which left the parents completely out of the picture. Mrs. Fenn's statement merely made it complicated and it was dismissed as 'not relevant'. And that is a great pity, because taking this statement seriously would have changed the entire case. For at least nine witnesses appear to have lied about their activities that Tuesday evening of May 1. As a result, the entire scenario as described above may well have happened. In any case there is nothing in the PJ files to contradict that the first scenario, where Kate leaves the Tapas bar before 21.30h, would be impossible. It would certainly explain the vacated chair and the empty plate but the PJ did not take any notice of this testimony and as far as is known, neither did Scotland Yard. It appears to be a recurring theme in the case: independent witnesses are not taken seriously whilst the entire Tapas group, including Gerry and Kate, can serve up stories or explanations which are accepted as the truth with little or no further investigation. Whilst the Tapas group can hardly be seen as independent witnesses and who could have their own reasons to be 'economical' with the truth or simply to remain silent about some matters. Apart from that some important statements contradict each other. But it seems the PJ has not noticed this. Consequently it wasn't long before any investigation into the statements of both Mrs. Fenn and Miss Chekaya was dropped and no serious further action was taken to find out what actually happened that Tuesday evening. At the same time it becomes clear that the investigators have no interest in scenarios other than a [paedophile] burglar; they appeared only to be interested in statements which included such individuals, which made them miss the importance of certain significant statements.

As described above, Tuesday evening the first of May is of crucial importance. For conflicting statements were recorded which should have been thoroughly investigated. For in this case only one of two answers would be the right one: on Tuesday May 1st at 23.00h Gerry and Kate were in the apartment or they were not. No other options are on the table. An important question that arises from all this: was there already a reason to mislead on Tuesday? It certainly looks that way.

11. THE 12-SECOND PHONE CALL

The situation around 11.45h on the morning of that fateful day, Thursday May 3, was as follows: after the various activities that morning the members of the Tapas group gathered around the swimming pool. They sat close together and talked about the their activities that morning. This was the first such gathering that week. David and Fiona hadn't returned from their morning sail this early; usually they only arrived back at the resort around 12.30h and collected their children from the crèche to have their lunch together. But now they'd returned about an hour earlier than they normally did. Russell and Jane, Matthew and Rachel and Gerry and Kate were all seated by the swimming pool. This 'morning meeting' of the group, as mentioned before, hadn't happened earlier that week and is for that reason worthy of some attention. For there is something else that stands out, namely that Gerry had his phone with him which had been switched off since 20.15h the previous day. So one has to ask: why did he take the phone with him? Did he need to call someone? That doesn't seem likely because the Vodafone records reveal that Gerry didn't ring anyone during that period. So it does not appear to have been the case that Gerry had arranged to phone someone that morning at a certain time. It seems that instead he was waiting for a call and that was why he took his mobile with him to the gathering at the swimming pool. There is no other obvious reason to do so. This is more than mere speculation, for Gerry did indeed receive a phonecall whilst there, exactly at 12.24'40h. He answered the call and the conversation is terminated at 12.24'52h and the connection is broken. So this was a 'conversation' lasting 12 seconds. It is not known what was discussed during this call, but then 12 seconds isn't a lot of time to have any kind of conversation. It looks more like a quick and short piece of information passed on than a normal phonecall. Also Gerry must have had some reason to expect the call in order to switch on his mobile and take it with him to the pool. And apart from the voicemails on the previous day it is the only call

Gerry will receive or make between 17.00h on Sunday the 29th April and 23.14h on Thursday the 3rd of May. So the situation seems to be as follows: during his holiday Gerry gets a phonecall from 'somebody' who then has a mere 12 seconds to speak to him. That is strange. You don't phone someone who is on holiday unless it is so urgent that it cannot wait a few days. It seems that 12 seconds is nowhere near enough time to discuss anything much, not even the weather. Over and out? That simply isn't logical. Of course you can make a mountain out of a molehill but all the same, there are a number of events which merited further investigation, simply because they are unusual and difficult to explain. For the call at 12.24h that afternoon seems to have triggered a rather large number of changes in the normal daily routine of the entire Tapas group. Another interesting point is that the statements regarding their activities and the times these took place vary wildly and a sort of collective amnesia seems to have overcome all members of the group, resulting in statements which contradicted each other. Conflicting statements which should not have been signed off or overlooked and moreover, which only arise from the events of that Thursday afternoon; for the statements regarding the days leading up to Thursday are reasonably consistent and appear to correspond with each other. But by Thursday afternoon all bets are off. David Payne tells the police that he doesn't know much about Thursday afternoon, really can't remember a lot. And Matthew too has lost most of that Thursday afternoon, as he tells the police, apart from his involuntary dip in the Atlantic Ocean during his sailing trip with Russell. Both men managed to fill dozens of pages about irrelevant recollections which were apparently still fresh in their minds. Another clear example of these contradictions can be found in the statements from Fiona Payne and Kate and Gerry as to who collected Madeleine from the crèche on Thursday afternoon. It is an important example because it concerns Madeleine. But who picked her up from the crèche? Fiona tells us in her rogatory interview on April 10th 2008: "... and then it was time to pick up the kids [..] and she [Kate] picked up Madeleine and I picked up Scarlet and then we walked back together and that was the only day we ever did, did that.' So much for Fiona Payne. And then there is Kate's own statement on 6th September 2007: quote '... when her lesson ended at 10.15h, she went to the recreation area next to the swimming pool to talk to Russell until Gerry's lesson was over. Afterwards, she is not sure, they went back together to the apartment until close to 12.15h when she went to Madeleine's crèche to pick her up, together with Fiona Payne [..] and went to the twins' crèche with the intention of picking them up, she thought she would meet Gerry there, not knowing if he already had the twins with him. Together with the three children she went to the apartment for lunch, with food bought at the supermarket.' End quote. As if this isn't confusing enough Gerry's statement of the 10th of May 2007 tells us: 'The tennis class finished at 11.15h, he stayed in the pool area talking with his wife and other persons, whom he does not remember. At 12.00h he agreed with Kate, as he recalls it, that she would make lunch and he would collect Madeleine. He thinks that it was Kate who took the twins home. Since it was he who went to collect Madeleine, he is sure he used the shortcut. At 12.30h they started lunch…' And that's it, three people and three different accounts about something so simple as picking up the children from the crèche. All this seems to have been triggered by the 12.24h phone call. So it is important to find out who the caller was who had set all this in motion. The Portuguese police does not appear to have tracked down the owner of this phone number, but independent research resulted in a positive identification. It turned out to be a colleague of Gerry who also works at the Leicester Hospital and at that time was a doctor, but by now is a professor. For reasons of privacy his name is, for now, Professor X. Obviously they knew each other from working at the hospital, but it appears that they both studied medicine in Glasgow; although they weren't fellow students, i.e. in the same year; they both specialized more or less in the same discipline of cardiovascular science. Professor X is older than Gerry and he is involved in scientific research. Even though his name isn't mentioned at all in the investigation, he is a person of interest because his actions give rise to a number of questions. Questions which haven't been asked so far and therefore there are no answers to be analyzed. So it is still not known what was said during that short, 12-second phone call. Surely it must be in Professor X's interest that there is nothing to connect him to the disappearance of Madeleine McCann. Answering the question as to what was said during that mysterious call could remove any hint of his involvement in the case. At least, depending on what Professor X will tell us. Even now, twelve years later, the question can still be asked, if only to have a complete record of what all the witnesses have stated at various times. One more statement added to the enormous body of information in this case wouldn't matter. And it's possible that Professor X may have some interesting information. However, it appears that the 12-second phone call was the only traceable contact between Gerry and Professor X from Leicestershire. This book covers the four months following the disappearance and despite all the stress and misery the McCanns had to cope with, Professor X appears not to have contacted the McCanns again, either by telephone or sms. Further independent research revealed that Professor X didn't use his private mobile number or indeed his office phone at the Leicester Hospital or his own landline number at home to contact Gerry. Not at all. And this seems a little odd. Surely it's what one expects: a quick call to a colleague who is going through a bad time, to buck him up at bit, possibly something like a sms, 'keep your spirits up' or 'stay positive'. But nothing of the sort happens. Professor X appears to ignore Gerry completely, it's as he doesn't exist. And that is surely a little surreal. One could certainly expect a bit more compassion from a close colleague. That is, unless Professor X was already aware of Madeleine's fate. For in that case sending messages of sympathy and support would be ridiculous. For if he knew that the situation could never have a positive ending, sending a message saying 'keep your spirits up' would be absurd. No, instead Professor X seems to have kept the McCanns at arm's length and had no contact with them whatsoever during all those months. But clearly the relationship was such that there was no problem if Professor X wanted to phone Gerry whilst he was enjoying his holiday, but not when that same colleague's daughter has been abducted. In fact he used his private mobile for this 12.24h call but after that not even one sms or phonecall from Professor X. Did he have a special reason to keep clear of the McCanns? In fact the 12-second call is the first and up to now only concrete proof that Gerry and Professor X were in contact with each other at all whilst Gerry was in Portugal. But at that point Madeleine hadn't disappeared, so what was the subject of that short conversation? It is a legitimate question and it should have been asked, but this never happened simply because the police officers of the PJ had been unable to trace the caller, Professor X. It needs to be said emphatically that, at this time, there's no evidence that Professor X had anything to do with the disappearance. But he should certainly have been interviewed for that 12-second call on the day of the disappearance because it is too conspicuous to ignore, it deserves further investigation. Even now. It appears after further independent research that it isn't Gerry but Russell O'Brien who before 2007 had a close working relationship with this Professor X. As early as the year 2000 Russell is doing research with him. After that he worked with the professor in a clinical science study in 2002, in one clinical study in 2003 and at least two clinical studies in 2007. If Professor X indeed played a [small] role in the disappearance, it's most likely that Russell made the initial contact with him.

12. THE POOL PHOTO

Of course it is impossible to write a book about the disappearance of Madeleine McCann without dedicating a chapter to the infamous 'pool photo'. For much has been written and debated concerning this photo and there is indeed a lot that is simply 'wrong' with it. It has to be said: the photograph has very probably been cobbled together by a well-meaning amateur, who was not fully familiar with the software programme he was using. A closer analysis reveals that mistake after mistake was made and the suggestion that the photograph was created by the British Secret Service is absolutely ridiculous. If the 'Section Forgeries' of MI5 and MI6 produced work of this level the entire staff would have been locked in the Tower of London, so to speak. It is almost certain that this picture was not 'photoshopped' by a professional illustrator or photographer, it is simply not good enough. Which takes us to the possibility that Gerry did it himself at the end of May 2007 when he was in the UK for a few days. But that seems to be a very simple explanation and probably not the right one. For although the photograph wasn't done by a professional, the chance that Gerry could get to grips with the techniques required in just an afternoon isn't very high. Although it isn't 'rocket science' it takes time and effort to understand and apply the tools Photoshop provides. There are no indications that Gerry was an enthusiastic photographer or that he would have had any reason to be familiar with professional photo software such as Photoshop.

Having said this, if the above is true it means that there was somebody in the UK at that time who actually did 'construct' this photograph. As it is not likely that Gerry did it himself, this means that somewhere there was a third party in the mix, somebody who fixed it for him. And has never said a word about it. But who could that be?

Well, let's see what's wrong with the image. For a start, the composition, it isn't natural. One would expect that Kate, who took the photograph, would have located the group in the centre of the image, just the way every tourist composes his or her holiday snaps. But she doesn't do that. What is also strange is that Sean isn't in the shot. What can have been the reason for his absence? Wouldn't it have been a lovely family photograph, Gerry and his three children sitting at the edge of the pool? But where is Sean? Was he standing next to Kate when she pressed the button? If that's the case, why not tell him to join his siblings by the edge of the pool? That would have made the picture complete. But apart from Sean not being there, the picture 'looks wrong'. Madeleine is apparently laughing and looking to her left, Amelie seems to be lost in her own little world and is looking down and Gerry looks straight into the lens of Kate's camera. That surely is a strange way to take a family picture on holiday. Normally what you do is tell them that they've all got to look at you and smile or wave. Surely that's the way one takes holiday snaps of one's family and friends? But clearly not as far as Kate is concerned. Consequently other points of interest present themselves.

Point 1: Looking closer at the photo it appears that there are large areas of shadow underneath the white loungers behind Gerry and on his T-shirt. This gives us the direction of the sun at the time, from the front and to Gerry's right. This means amongst other factors that there should be shadows behind his legs and the hand that is resting on the edge of the pool, but strangely enough, this is not the case. This lack of shadow also gives Gerry the appearance of 'floating' above the edge of the swimming pool. That is remarkable. Point 2: In addition there is another shadow on Gerry's body which gives rise to more questions. On his left on his thigh and on his shorts a large dark shadow is clearly visible, but it is not clear how this is possible, knowing that the sun is in front of him to his right. This shadow does not belong in the scene. Point 3: Near there, behind Amelie, between her left arm and her body a small and mysterious black line can be seen. What is it? And what is it doing there? It does not belong in the background and looks very much as if it is the remains of a sloppy 'copy-paste' effort by an amateur. Yet another indication that the photograph was 'processed' and this in any case remarkable Point 4.

Next we have Gerry's sunglasses, what's wrong with them? They look very unreal, the size and glitter in the lenses; the sunglasses look as if they are floating just in front of his face. Over the years people have debated this effect and have produced extensive and scientific investigations dealing with the reflection of the sun in the lenses, with the result that they came to the conclusion that Gerry wasn't wearing the sunglasses when Kate took the photograph, but they were 'pasted' in at a later date. Point 5: And all that after taking a good look at a holiday snap, an innocent looking family scene by the edge of a swimming pool. The sort of photograph pretty well all of us have taken at one time or another. How remarkable can those be? Or is it the case that once again these things only happen to the McCanns? We can conclude that the 'pool photo' is almost certainly a fake. This leads us to the next question: why was it necessary to manipulate this photograph? Why was so much effort made to produce this photo for the media? Is it in fact a statement, a sort of silent message from the McCanns? Something like, whatever anyone says, Gerry, the children and Kate were at the swimming pool at exactly 14.29h and therefore none of us could have been anywhere else? And this photograph is the absolute proof, something like that. In any case the photo is the only 'evidence' which places the McCann family at the swimming pool that Thursday afternoon. So to prove that the image was photoshopped is very important. For along with that, the so-called proof of the presence of the family at that time and place disappears, leaving a gap in time during which they were otherwise engaged. Knowing this, what can be the reason why the world had to believe that the family was at the pool whilst that was patently untrue? And perhaps even more important: if they weren't at the swimming pool, where were they? And why did that have to be a secret? It must have been important to Gerry, taking into account the lengths he had to go to in order to produce the photograph. And there's yet another factor concerning this 'holiday snap'. Gerry brought the photograph with him on the 22nd of May from the UK when he'd spent a few days at home. Both the McCanns were very keen to let the world know that the photograph had been taken exactly at 14.29h on Thursday. The time in particular appeared to be important to them. The question remains: why was it so very important to have everyone believe that the photograph was taken exactly at 14.29h? Was it to prove that Madeleine was still alive? That she was healthy and happy at that time? Not exactly, but surely that was a bonus. [In fact it was Gerry's alibi for that afternoon.]

Continuously stressing the exact time the photo was taken leads one to suspect that the photo wasn't taken at that time at all, but provided some kind of alibi for the McCanns, or for Gerry, to cover other activities that took place that afternoon. It is almost impossible for the McCann family to have been at the swimming pool at 14.29h that Thursday afternoon. For if they had been there they could just have taken [not one but several] holiday snaps without there being any question whether the resulting images were 'real'. But it is no longer in doubt that the photograph is photoshopped. So what are the first questions that should logically be asked? Where were the McCanns if they were not at the swimming pool? And why did that have to be a secret? And why was it so very important to Gerry to tell and show the world that he was, together with his family, at the swimming pool at 14.29h exactly? Why was it also so important for Gerry to produce that 'solid' proof? It had to be some sort of alibi for him, that's the reason that this photo suddenly appeared. This means the entire family McCann disappears from the radar; nobody knows what they actually did do, or where they have been. If Gerry had something else to do that afternoon without anyone knowing, he seems to have succeeded. For that afternoon he was 'invisible' between 12.30h to 15.30h, until he joined Kate for their tennis lesson together. It was tennis coach Dan Stuk, who was the first independent witness to see him [and Kate] that afternoon around 15.30h on the tennis court.

13. MATTHEW AND RUSSELL'S SAILING ADVENTURE

The main aim of the police when questioning a witness is to find out the truth. Determine what has happened, under which circumstances, with whom and by whom, in order to get to the truth. It is not at all advisable to let a witness ramble on without interruption or to ask the witness for further details. Not only that, the police officer conducting the interview should listen very carefully and take particular note of the choice of words used by the witness. After all, a witness can easily become a suspect. It stands to reason that interviewing witnesses is only useful if one has a critical attitude analyzing the statements made. And if there are contradictions with other statements or facts known to the police during the interview, it is best to react to the discrepancy immediately by posing another question regarding that particular subject. For this to be the case, the interviewing officer must know the case files very well indeed. For only by asking the witness more questions regarding a doubtful statement will it be possible to obtain more information from the witness. Apart from that and not at all unimportant, one has to keep analyzing the statement made by the witness. Is it a logical story? Is it realistic? Is it at all credible? Imagine that a witness states that he has climbed Mount Everest in four hours, a police officer can take this down without thinking further about the statement, but that doesn't mean it can be believed. For it is in no way a credible story and therefore not to be believed. One may assume that it is generally known that Mount Everest is the highest mountain in the world and that it takes a lot longer than four hours to climb it. To write this down without reacting to this obviously impossible statement means that it will remain in the file without being ever questioned or noticed. Clearly the 'mountaineer' witness had his reasons to give this nonsensical explanation and therefore it is very important to find out why. Knowingly telling lies as a witness is not allowed and against the law. Not only that, the witness is to be regarded with suspicion. Clearly it's most important to establish what the reason for the 'lie' may have been. But all this will come to nothing if the interviewing officer doesn't carefully consider what is being said. The realistic probability of the statement is not tested by asking more questions.

In the Madeleine investigation by the PJ mistakes such as the one described above appear fairly often. Simply writing down what the witness says without thinking about the credibility of the statements and without noticing contradictions which require further investigation. A good example are the statements made by Matthew Oldfield and Russell O'Brien regarding their sailing trip the afternoon of May 3rd, the day Madeleine disappeared. Both men had decided to take a catamaran out for an afternoon's sail. Matthew Oldfield is an experienced sailor but Russell O'Brien decidedly not. More importantly: he doesn't know anything about sailing, leave alone sailing a boat on his own. Keeping in mind that apart from that, not knowing anything about sailing, a catamaran is far more difficult to control than a standard sailing boat. A catamaran with its two parallel hulls is lightweight and very difficult to steer as it has a tendency to capsize. Even an experienced sailer would initially have trouble controlling a catamaran. What follows is what apparently happened that Thursday afternoon. At least, according to Matthew Oldfield and Russell O'Brien. Both men told the police the same story: they had decided to 'take a catamaran out' to have a sail that afternoon. Everything went well until Matthew, of the two men the experienced sailor, fell overboard into the ocean. This made Russell automatically captain and forced him to sail the catamaran all by himself. Matthew, still in the ocean, doubted whether Russell could get him back on board and he calculated how far he was from the coast. He estimated it was about a mile. Matthew then thought, as he told the police, that in the worst case he must swim all the way to the beach. But the last thing he'd expected happened; Russell managed to turn the catamaran round and picked him up, managing not to sail right over him, something that had worried him rather, as Matthew says in his statement. Later both men had a good laugh about it and told their partners all about the sailing adventure. The entire group found the story hilarious, mainly because the experienced sailor Matthew was the one who'd fallen in the ocean and 'rookie' Russell who had saved him. It's indeed a jolly good story but it raises more questions than it answers and deserves closer scrutiny. Unfortunately this didn't happen and so two statements have been included in the files which have not been questioned or critically evaluated.

In this book their statements will be critically examined. For a start 'taking a catamaran out'. Their statements indicate that they were free to 'take' a catamaran to have a sail on the ocean. This, however, is not how it's done. Sailing vessels, surfboards and so on are rented out by a firm named Beach Hut Watersports situated on the beach of Praia da Luz. Before the staff of Beach House Watersports allow a catamaran to be taken out, the prospective clients are asked for information on their experience sailing the specific craft they have selected and after they're instructed on how to deal with the craft. Wind direction, wind speed, the currents and the weather forecast for the day are discussed. After all, one is going to sail on the Atlantic Ocean and not on an inland lake. The prospective client is asked how familiar he is with the vessel he wants to rent, specifically a catamaran, since this type of vessel is difficult to handle. But nowhere in the statements of Oldfield or O'Brien is it clear that they have indeed had such a briefing. The impression is given that they could simply 'take' the catamaran and take it to the ocean without help or advice from third parties.

A little further in his statement Matthew states that he fell off the boat; he suddenly finds himself in the Atlantic Ocean whilst Russell, now all alone on the boat, is rapidly sailing away from him. Matthew thinks that Russell won't be able to pick him up with the catamaran and he expects that he will have to swim to the coast, about a mile away as he calculated. But that seems very optimistic. For what stands out in this story is that Matthew doesn't mention once in what a dangerous and life-threatening situation he found himself. What is also remarkable is that Matthew says absolutely nothing about how cold the water he'd been plunged into actually was. According to local meteorological data the water temperature of the ocean that day was 12–13 degrees Celsius and that is undoubtedly cold. Compared to Matthew's body temperature this gives a difference of 24 degrees Celsius. This difference is enormous and therefore very dangerous. The body will protest forcibly against this sudden drop in temperature, with the direct and inevitable result that the cold forces the swimmer to breathe fast and in short bursts, gasping for air. Moreover, body heat is lost in no time in such a situation, causing muscles to contract leading to severe cramps. [A body loses heat in water twenty-five times faster than in the air.] This is the start of severe hypothermia which is life-threatening in water of this temperature. For the danger is that the combination of short and fast breathing and the immersion in very cold water will lead to 'cold shock' and due to the great difference in temperature of the body and the cold water, the chance of heart failure leading to drowning is very great. This process would have given Matthew in the circumstances he found himself in, no more than thirty minutes to live. In other words: Matthew Oldfield had a big problem, a problem which could cost him his life. His body would stop to function due to hypothermia. And apparently he thought he could save himself by swimming? [As it happens the last thing one should do in such a situation]. He estimated the distance to the coast to be about a mile and expected to have to swim that distance. This is indeed what he later told the police. But this is not a realistic scenario; a mile from the coast is quite a distance to swim and apart from that it's not so simple to do this in the Atlantic Ocean with an offshore wind force four to five. Most certainly not in cold water without any protective clothing. But even with half a wetsuit on it remains a very dangerous situation. Even though Matthew says he can swim that distance, it is the same as the mountaineer climbing Mount Everest; it is impossible that he would make it, the distance is simple too great, his body would have stopped functioning due to hypothermia before he would have had time to cover that distance of a mile to the coast. Even with some protective clothing. Knowing this, isn't it very curious that he doesn't say anything at all about this? Not a single word? He is a doctor and one may assume that he would therefore know about the dangers of hypothermia and what that does to a human body. In other words: when he was plunged into the very cold water he should have realized immediately that he was in grave danger. But he says absolutely nothing about this in his statement to the police and that seems rather strange. Wouldn't it have been worth mentioning? That he'd cheated death and that the little sailing trip could have turned into a tragedy? Moreover, that the day was saved through Russell's heroic efforts? That would certainly have been an interesting story? But no, nothing in any of the statements, whilst many might think Russell deserves a medal. For what he has managed to do is far more than heroic. Never having sailed so much as a sailboat, leave alone a fast and lightweight catamaran and yet he succeeded in turning the boat and pick up Matthew without capsizing or sailing right over him. To make it clear how brilliantly Russell has performed we have to go back to that Thursday afternoon the third of May: according to the meteorological data the wind that afternoon was offshore, force four to five. For sailors this means that this is a good wind and one could sail as a 'sport' rather than just for fun. Also don't forget that this is on the Atlantic Ocean. So: Russell sees Matthew falling off the boat and knew apparently immediately what he had to do by grabbing the wheel and adjust the right lines of the sail. At least, he must have done so just to be able to steer the boat. He looks back and sees Matthew in the water, getting smaller and smaller because of the turn of speed of the catamaran. But he doesn't panic, apparently not. Russell never mentioned any such thing, but surely his heart must have been beating faster when he was so suddenly left alone on the catamaran, in the middle of the ocean. Surely he would have been very worried and have wondered how on earth he could get back to the shore from where they came; it isn't exactly a car where you can simply throw the steering wheel round and do a three point turn. No, the wind has an important role in sailing and then there is the direction of the prevailing wind. The typical techniques used such as

'Close Hauled', 'Come About' and 'Luffing' are completely foreign to Russell, but still he miraculously managed to turn the catamaran round. That is despite a brisk wind, not knowing anything at all about sailing, without any experience of being on a ship of any kind and yet without capsizing, he managed to steer the boat in a very short time back to Matthew who was adrift in the Atlantic Ocean. Who climbed back on board without any trouble? This would be no less than a scene from an action movie. And that actual 'picking up' of Matthew? Don't forget that Matthew has already been immersed in very cold water for some time and it would be hard for him to move quickly. He would be moving with some effort and to grab one of the hulls of the catamaran, as it passes by, and climb on top of it would be very hard. Hypothermic reaction would already have set in and affected the strength of his arm muscles, all of which would make it extremely difficult for him to grab and hold on to the passing catamaran steered by Russell. How on earth did he do that? Of course there are several ways to decrease the speed of the boat and to get someone aboard in full sea but how could Russell know any of these techniques? And even then, how could he execute these so perfectly with a difficult to steer, light and fast catamaran? Another interesting omission is that Matthew never mentions the life jacket which he surely must have been wearing. Nothing about this in his statement that 'luckily he was wearing a life jacket'. He doesn't say either that it was very difficult to swim with a life jacket on, certainly if you are a mile from shore ploughing through the waves with frozen arms it's pretty well impossible. But all that ends, ends well for Matthew as he managed to grab hold of the boat and climb back on board, still not hampered by wearing a clumsy life jacket. Once back on board nothing happens, according to the statements of both men. And that too is strange. For what they should have mentioned at the very least is that they immediately went back to the coast and the beach. Why? Certainly because Matthew would have suffered from hypothermia and because his body temperature wouldn't just go back to 37 degrees Celsius just because he was no longer in cold water. The air temperature was around 19 degrees Celsius and that was nowhere near enough to warm him up. The fresh 'sporty' wind wouldn't help either. A body dressed in wet clothes cools down five times faster than when wearing dry clothes. But there is nothing in the statements about these problems. In fact, even though back on board, Matthew is still in danger despite being out of the ocean. Russell should have rubbed him warm with his bare hands or with a towel if it was available. [Who would meanwhile be sailing the boat in that case?] But not a word about this in the statements. No mention either of Matthew shivering and shaking with cold on the catamaran. But if Matthew had really fallen off the catamaran that is exactly what would have happened.

We have more than enough reasons to doubt this story. It simply doesn't ring true. And the diligent police taking all this down, apparently without a grain of suspicion, never considering whether this was a realistic scenario. Matthew who experienced a life threatening situation without even mentioning it and Russell who had miraculous powers of sailing a catamaran with wind force four to five on the Atlantic Ocean without ever having done so before. Does this sound like a credible account? It is definitely important to establish whether or not this event took place. If not it means that witness Oldfield and witness O'Brien must have had a reason to construct a story about what took place that Thursday afternoon on the ocean. And that is exactly what witnesses are not meant to do, constructing stories, which is in fact downright lying. But what could be the reason to dream up this impossible event? This last question is very important, but was unfortunately never put to the two witnesses because no critical analysis of the statements of both men was undertaken. The contradictions in their story in fact reveal how unlikely it is that the event took place at all. It is quite incredible that this was not spotted by the police investigators and for this reason they were never questioned further. It looks very much as a fictitious story made up by the two men. Matthew didn't fall off the boat, for then he would have felt quite differently about his unplanned dive in the ocean and would most certainly not have laughed it off. His life was in serious danger in the cold water and hypothermia was an absolutely certain consequence. But at that moment it happened we have to believe that he never thought of that fact when he fell off the boat into a very cold ocean? When he started to get short of breath? No panic at all? A good mile from the coast? Knowing that Russell can't sail at all? Hard to believe, but apparently not, for he never mentions any of this in his statement. Surely he must have had a terrible shock and have feared for his life, so why shouldn't he say so? And then Russell, who can suddenly sail a catamaran and steer it where he wants? Without any instructions? On the Atlantic Ocean? Is this credible? There are too many factors which do not ring true and are indeed not logical. The question arises: why did they invent such a story if it never happened? Two adult men, doctors even, what reason may they have had? Surely not to appear to be heroes to impress their nearest and dearest? It is clear that the statements made by witness Oldfield and witness O'Brien regarding the events during the sailing trip on that Thursday afternoon are, to put it mildly, 'difficult' to believe. But why was it at all necessary to construct a story? For something so much fun and innocent as an afternoon's sailing? The answer to this question is clear and surprising and will be discussed in a later chapter of this book. ['The Invisible Men']

To understand exactly what a terrible experience it must have been for Matthew when he fell into the cold water of the ocean here follows an detailed description about hypothermia and how the body reacts to it. It will be patently obvious that Matthew, because he never mentions any of these serious consequences, has clearly made the whole thing up. At the very least he should have mentioned how the cold water seemed to paralyze his arms and legs and how his body reacted to the disastrous situation he found himself in. But instead he serves up a rather nonchalant story, forgetting to add any of these pertinent details, clearly because it never happened. Next is set out what would definitely have happened to his body if he'd fallen into the very cold water of the ocean.

Whatever situation or the location, the human body will always do what it can to keep the 'core temperature' at 37 degrees Celsius. This is essential, dropping or raising the temperature by just a few degrees can be fatal. If the core temperature drops the internal organs will not function. If a 'warm' body is in danger of hypothermia an automatic survival system kicks in by pumping large amounts of adrenaline through the body. This will stimulate the cells to generate energy [heat] far more quickly than would normally be the case. In cold water this internal defense of the body will prove to be fruitless; a body in cold water cools down twenty-five times faster than in air. The body heat dissipates in the surrounding water. It is a fact that when a body is immersed in very cold water a life or death situation is in progress. 'Cold shock' can occur, the heart simply stops under the stress and one drowns. But before this happens one's toes and fingers will go numb and it will be harder breathe. The body is literally 'losing it': it wants more oxygen, blood vessels contract to counter heat loss and the heart is beating as fast as it can. Then the body will start shaking uncontrollably, another desperate effort of the body to rid itself of the cold that is assaulting it. But just this effort leads the body to poison itself with the carbon dioxide produced by the involuntary trembling and shaking which raises the acid level of the blood. This is a very dangerous situation indeed. Even a very small raise in acidity can lead to total organ failure and death. To avoid this happening the brain gets a signal which has the result that the body starts to breathe faster and much deeper than normal in order to eliminate the carbon dioxide from the blood. All these defense mechanisms are entirely concerned with maintaining the 'core temperature'. But in the end the cold water will win this fight, despite all efforts, the 'core temperature' cannot be maintained and fatal hypothermia is the inevitable outcome.*

Photo: Beach Hut Watersports

An exact copy of the catamaran that Russell and Matthew
allegedly sailed on Thursday afternoon May 3.

Photo: Peter Scharrenberg

A traffic sign in Praia da Luz that clearly tells the general
feeling of the people of the small village.

Photo: Kate McCann

The infamous pool photo that Kate took on Thursday afternoon at 14.29h. [At least that's what she said.] But there are some serious contradictions in the photo. A: there is shadow under the sun bed but, B, not behind Gerry's right leg on the edge of the pool. C: there is a strange shadow on Gerry's upper left leg that is not consistent with the other shadows in the picture. And D: between Amelie's arm and her body there is a curious black stripe visible that doesn't belong there. Gerry's sun glasses look odd, concerning the reflection of the sun. A lot of irregularities in a simple holiday picture.

Photo: Kate McCann

A very clear indication that this photo was falsified is the absence of the right arm of Amelie. The position of the short sleeve points in such a direction that one may expect that her right arm would be visible, but it is not. So where is her right arm?

On page 1592, a divulgation, appealing to the person who on the 3rd of May 2007, at around 9.30 p.m., in Praia da Luz, transported a child in his arms, to identify himself, in order to dismiss the situation that was narrated by witness JANE TANNER.

Further on this issue, the testimony of **MARTIN SMITH** was considered, pages 1606 and following, reporting the sighting of an individual carrying a child, in one of the streets that lead to the beach. It was said that the child could be **MADELEINE McCANN**, although it was never peremptorily stated. Some time later, the witness alleged that, by its stance, the individual who carried the child could be **GERALD McCANN**, which was concluded when he saw him descending the stairs from an airplane, pages 2871, 3991 and following and 4135 and following. It was established that at the time that was being mentioned, **GERALD McCANN** was sitting at the table, in the Tapas Restaurant.

The works that carried out construction works in Vila da Luz were heard, pages 1650 and 18..., who did not detect anything strange, during their works of excavation and placement of plumbing (also see pages 3983 to 3987), although they carefully verified, on the day that followed the disappearance and before they started the works, if there was a body hidden next to said works.

From pages 1811 to 1827 we appended two lab tests and the corresponding reports, which turned out to have no evidential interest for

Source: PJ files

The official translation of the Portuguese final report which contains a crucial error. There were in fact two Tapas employees who have stated that Gerry was not in the restaurant for half an hour, in a critical time period on the evening that Madeleine disappeared.

Inquiries were made that led to the identification of an English individual, with a criminal background, namely in crimes of a sexual nature, and who was the target of various inquiries without incriminatory results. Inquiries of the same kind were made with regard to other individuals, without yielding any results of interest to the investigation, as can be found in Apense VI.

A situation was investigated relating to two individuals, Neil B. and Rajinder B., especially as regards the former, whose information was crossed with Tasmin Silence's witness account, the photofit showing that this was not the same individual. In spite of the inquiries made, including by means of the Letter of Request, nothing was found to link him to the disappearance of the British girl.

Martin Smith was questioned, who said that at the beginning of the Travessa da Escola Primária he saw an individual carrying a child, walking in the opposite direction, at a normal pace, when he passed this individual it must have been about 22.00, being totally unaware that a child had disappeared. Later he states that when he saw Gerald McCann on the news, leaving by plane, he appeared to him to be the individual whom he had seen on the night of 3rd May in Praia da Luz.

This witness was heard again by the Drogheda Irish police on 23-01-08, having been shown a video clip of Gerald McCann's departure by plane carrying one of the twins. This witness maintains his belief that judging by the posture, there seemed to be a probability of 60-80% that ~~the person seen by him at about 21.55 at the previously mentioned place, was Madeleine's father~~ At this time, Gerald's presence at the restaurant was confirmed by his friends and has not been denied by restaurant employees.

The sighting in Mem Martins on 11-06-2007 is also mentioned and was found not to be truthful.

Hoos Hendrik, owner of an animal crematorium, appeared before the PJ, to clarify that he had nothing to do with the disappearance, contrary to insinuations that had been made.

Fls 3447 contains information provided by the Spanish agency Método 3, that in Vale Barrigas, Sao Bartolomeu de Messines – IC – km 71 7.4 a witness saw a woman hand a blanket wrapped bundle to a man over a 160 cm high metal fence. The woman seen next to the car was similar to Michaela Walczuch: however, from an analysis of mobile phone activity and the activation of antennas, it can be seen that on 4th May 2007, between 15.00 and 17.00, Robert Murat, Michaela Walczuch, Sergey Malinka and Luis Antonio were in the zones of Lagos, Porto de Mós, Penha, Alvor and Praia da Luz, all of these sites being located at a distance of more than 65 km from the place the witness refers to.

Source: PJ files

The same mistake appears in all known English translations.
'...has not been denied by restaurant employees.'

Photo: Peter Scharrenberg

The location where it all went wrong for Gerry: here he encountered
the Smith family from Ireland who were walking towards him and
had a good view of him and Madeleine. Their statements however
were ingnored by the PJ because 'it was established' that Gerry was in
the Tapas bar at the time the Smiths met 'the man with a child'.

Photo: Peter Scharrenberg

Rua das Flores, no 27, Vivenda Vista do Mar, Luz Park, Luz, Lagos.
This is the villa the McCanns rented after they left the 'Ocean Club'.

14. "WHY DIDN'T YOU COME?"

On Thursday morning the 3rd of May, the day of the disappearance, something unusual happened at breakfast in the McCann's apartment. That is, according to Kate who gave a statement to the police concerning this unusual event. And although breakfast is a normal daily routine, something happened which had not occurred before, which made this breakfast 'special' and unusual enough for Kate to make a statement. It concerns the fact that Madeleine, according to Kate, during breakfast asked why nobody had come to her room when Sean [or Amelie] was crying, as it had woken her up. This would have happened on the Wednesday night and at first it seems to be a perfectly normal question, but this is not really the case. In fact it is not at all a normal question and it is highly unlikely that Madeleine asked this question. First the explanation to support this firm conviction.

The situation at the time can be described as follows. As stated earlier, it was Thursday morning and the McCann family were seated at the table for breakfast. During the meal Madeleine tells her parents that she [last night] woke up because of one of her siblings was crying and that this had upset her. She asks her parents why nobody came to her room to stop either of he twins crying. Madeleine slept with her brother and sister in one room, she in a normal single bed and the twins each in a portable cot. Madeleine is talking about the Wednesday evening which is the evening the Tapas group, including her parents, had a drink at the bar of the restaurant and did not return to the apartment until around midnight. And here the statement of the upstairs neighbour, Mrs. Fenn, is of some importance: she stated that the parents returned home around 23.45h on the Tuesday night. And that she had heard a child crying from 22.30h until 23.45h that evening. The McCanns strongly denied this and said they were absolutely sure that Mrs. Fenn was mistaken in the day the crying occurred. It wasn't the Tuesday evening they returned to the apartment around midnight, but Wednesday evening. Yes, of course, one of our children might have cried one night, but that was definitely not the Tuesday, otherwise we'd have heard it, said the McCanns. For that evening they were back with the children around 23.00h, at least that's what they stated. However, exactly this insistence on the McCann version of events that Wednesday night creates doubts about Madeleine's alleged question at breakfast. One of the children may well have cried for an hour and fifteen minutes, but that must have been the Wednesday evening and not Tuesday evening. During the investigation questions were also asked by the police concerning Madeleine's sleep pattern. Was there anything they should know? Could she have gone for a walk and then been taken away by somebody? It seems far-fetched but the police was looking for anything that could result in a new direction to be followed up and investigated. The answers given by Gerry and Kate regarding her sleep patterns are very surprising and appear to confirm that the question allegedly asked by Madeleine was never asked. For what transpires? Madeleine did indeed have a history of waking up during the night. She would then always go the her parents and sleep the rest of the night with them. Special training with appropriate rewards given changed this undesirable behaviour, at least according to Kate. And also, Madeleine had never, either in the evening or at night, left the house on her own to go for a walk.

This is Kate's statement, given when she was an 'arguido' [a word used for a suspect], during her interview by the PJ on the 6th September 2007:
10-PROCESSO 10 VOLUME Xa (Pages 2539 to 2551)
Kate Marie Healy's statement 06/09/07 at 3.00 p.m.

Quote: 'Regarding a British custom of having a behaviour chart for the children, she says that she has several notes about Madeleine because with some regularity she gets up during the night. This situation was reported from April 2006 up to her birthday that same year, when she stopped having this problem. These notes correspond to the stars given on the nights Madeleine did not get up and go to her parents' room. When she had twenty stars she got a present and if she woke up at night and did not stay in her bed, she did not get a star. When asked about the fact that her daughter had been crying on the night of the Tuesday for one hour and fifteen minutes, between 22.30h and 23.45h, Kate says it is not true. She says that on that night, after midnight, Madeleine went to their room and said that her sister Amelie was crying, and so she slept with her and Gerry in their bed. She says that before Madeleine appeared in their room she had already heard Amelie crying. However she did not go to the room, as Madeleine appeared in the parents room almost at the same time she heard the crying. She does not remember if afterwards she or Gerry went to the children's room, however she states that Amelie cried for a short time.' Unquote.

Loosely translated Kate says that it is a British custom to create a 'behaviour chart' for children and that this chart recorded the fact that Madeleine woke fairly regularly at night, she would then leave her bed and get in bed with her parents. By implementing this form of training and by rewarding her if appropriate, her sleep behaviour was corrected by April 2006. Kate goes on to say that she cannot remember whether the children woke at night during the holiday. However at home in the UK Madeleine would sometimes wake up and would then creep into her parents' bed. All according to Kate. And that is not quite all. For meanwhile both parents had stated that Madeleine had left her bed on the Tuesday night, had gone to their bedroom and had ended up sleeping in their bed for the rest of the night. She took this action because, according to Kate, her little sister Amelie had cried for 'a short time'. For this reason she went to another room, so the crying would not disturb her and she'd be able to sleep. Something that happens in many other family's with young children and is not at all unusual. All the same this information is important because it clearly is an indication of Madeleine's sleep pattern that week. Now we know that Madeleine had a history of waking at night and leaving her bed to go and sleep with her parents and that she did just that the day before for no other reason than that Amelie had cried for a short time. What does that mean regarding the credibility of what Kate in her interview on 6th September 2007 calls 'the crying episode'? Namely, Madeleine asking her parents on the Thursday morning why they didn't come when Sean or Amelie were crying? Can we derive something from this? Certainly we can. We can say, with a very high probability, that Madeleine didn't leave her bed on the Wednesday night, she must have stayed in bed. This, despite the fact that she herself was crying or Amelie or Sean was. [The statements vary as to which of the children were crying but this is not of prime importance here]. So Madeleine stayed in her bed, even when the crying went on for an hour and fifteen minutes, [as Kate said that Mrs. Fenn had heard this long period of crying on Wednesday night].

But is this really the truth? Probably not. Because it's highly unlikely that Madeleine would have patiently borne the long period of crying and stay in her own bed. According to Kate Madeleine had left her bed the previous evening because Amelie 'cried for a short time'. So is it possible that Madeleine listened to intense crying for well over an hour, or perhaps she herself was crying, but without leaving her bed and the room? Is this a reasonable conclusion, once one knows that she had woken the previous evening too and had gone to sleep with her parents? No, that is not a reasonable conclusion at all, it is of course possible but not at all likely. Yet she must have done exactly that, she stayed in bed and did not seek the comfort of sleeping with her parents, who were close by as she well knew. No, she stayed in bed, even when the crying had been going on for over an hour. This has to be the case, there is no doubt that Madeleine stayed in her bed, despite the continuous crying which stopped her from sleeping. For how can it be otherwise, the question she allegedly asked at breakfast on that Thursday morning is the proof. 'Why didn't you come to my room when I was crying last night? This implicates that she stayed in bed. Why? For the simple reason that if she had got out of bed and had gone to her parents' bedroom she would have seen that they were not in bed and neither were they anywhere in the apartment. This means that she would have asked a different question at breakfast on Thursday morning. Like: 'Why weren't you in bed last night when I was crying?' Or: 'Why weren't you there last night when I cried?' But she didn't ask those questions and therefore it is certain that Madeleine, entirely against her normal behaviour, did not leave her bed on Wednesday night. Did she really manage to stay in bed even after nearly an hour and a half of crying? It doesn't seem credible to take this as the truth, for what child would be able to endure such misery?

The question we should now ask is this: why did Kate invent this question Madeleine is supposed to have asked? For that is exactly what she must have done if Madeleine, as one might expect, would have got out of bed. In that case she could not have asked this question. But Kate stated that Madeleine definitely asked this question, but that she then just 'moved on'. This makes it almost certain that Madeleine didn't say anything during breakfast; she would otherwise have asked a different question altogether and that means without any doubt that Kate invented the whole episode. But why? Why would she give Madeleine a starring role at breakfast and invent a question she allegedly asked? Is it possible that she wanted to let others know that her eldest daughter was still alive on that Thursday morning? Could that be the reason? Was it important to create a role for Madeleine and a short conversation reported almost as an aside to the bigger events? What exactly did Gerry and Kate want to establish? Experience has taught us that when the McCanns insistently repeat or deny a statement it is often the case that the opposite is true. In other words: this again seems like an indication that Madeleine was no longer alive on Thursday morning. For the simple reason that the McCanns were producing 'evidence' to prove she was still alive at that point, even when at that time no-one doubted the abduction story. It is almost certainly a fact that Madeleine would have got out of bed that night and gone to her parents' bedroom to sleep with them, much as she was used to do.

79

It's not credible that she would have stayed such a long time in her own bed, she would, just like any other child, have gone to ask her parents to comfort her. Now that is logical behaviour one can expect from a child and surely one should expect the same reaction from Madeleine. The fact that she did not do this, at least according to the alleged question she asked, seems to indicate that something already had gone wrong with Madeleine. For why would she not behave exactly the same as any other three year old?

15. CUDDLECAT, WHAT HAPPENED?

If there was a magical spell that could make a cuddly toy talk, then it should be used on Madeleine's most favorite toy 'Cuddlecat'. For that was the toy that was left on the empty bed after Madeleine disappeared. According to Kate that was an indication, if not proof, that Madeleine had not voluntarily left the apartment for she would certainly have taken 'Cuddlecat' with her.

Kate's statement seems to be a perfectly logical conclusion but as is the case in nearly all of her statements, there is a very good reason to doubt her words. The officers of the PJ noticed when they did their first inspection of apartment 5A that the cuddly toy lay in a rather strange spot on the bed. 'Cuddlecat' lay next to the pillow at the head of the bed, very neatly posed on one side, just as if someone had put it there. It certainly didn't look as if a child had been sleeping with the toy close to her. The investigators of the PJ wrote this important information in their notebooks: 'strange position of cuddly toy on the bed'. Much later in the investigation the presence of the cuddly toy on the bed will grow into one of the greatest mysteries surrounding the disappearance, at least as far as the PJ and Scotland Yard are concerned. For what is the issue here? The situation is as follows: 'Cuddlecat' is found on Madeleine's bed in a strange position and appears to have been put there deliberately. Much later in the investigation Eddie, the sniffer dog who has been trained to detect 'cadaver odour', will mark 'Cuddlecat' as positive for this 'cadaver odour'. This means that the cuddly toy must have been in contact with a corpse or that somebody who has been in contact with a corpse has transferred this unpleasant odour to the cuddly toy. One of these two situations must have taken place, there are no other options. In this case it hardly matters which of the two options one chooses, it has suddenly become an inexplicable situation. For something is clearly wrong here. As a reminder: who is Eddie? At that time Eddie was a seven-year old male Springer Spaniel, trained as an Enhanced Victim Recovery Dog [EVRD]. Trained to detect human cadaver odour, either directly from the source, i.e. a corpse, or to react to cadaver odour which 'hangs around' even when a dead body is moved to another location. It is clear that Eddie had exceptional qualities.

Below a list of the locations and objects where this sniffer dog alerted positively, indicating 'cadaver odour' in and outside apartment 5A:

- Cadaver odour in apartment 5A, in the living room behind the sofa, under the window.
- Cadaver odour in apartment 5A, on the balcony near the parents' bedroom.
- Cadaver odour near apartment 5A, directly under the window of the parents'bedroom.
- Cadaver odour in apartment 5A, in the corner of a wardrobe in the parents' bedroom.
- Cadaver odour on the inside of the car door of the car rented by the McCanns.
- Cadaver odour on two items of clothing belonging to Kate.
- Cadaver odour on a t-shirt belonging to Madeleine's little brother Sean.
- Cadaver odour on Madeleine's favourite cuddly toy Cuddlecat.

Although this is a long list of positive alerts, one alert was not given by Eddie, namely, a positive alert on Madeleine's bed. Did he make a mistake? Wouldn't he have detected the scent? This last is very unlikely, not least because Eddie had a perfect track record, but also taking into account all the other objects and locations where he did signal the presence of cadaver odour. Therefore, with a probability verging on certainty it can be assumed that there was no cadaver odour on Madeleine's bed. And that is in fact quite impossible. Let's go back to that Thursday night. In the children's room Cuddlecat lies on the empty bed where until a very short time ago, Madeleine herself lay asleep, at least that is what Gerry and Kate claim. And then logically the next question is: how can there be cadaver odour on Cuddlecat but not on the bed on which it lay? Apparently there cannot have been a dead body in that bed, Madeleine's bed, for otherwise Eddie would have alerted to the scent. So obviously the logical questions are: where did Cuddlecat acquire the cadaver odour? And consequently who put the cuddly toy on the bed? And why? All these important questions required an answer, but unfortunately they were never asked. And as it took some time after the investigation with the CSI dogs for the forensic results to be processed, it was decided not to use these results as evidence but rather indicative of the direction the investigation should take. Even so, the questions remain: how did Cuddlecat acquire the cadaver odour and who put the toy on the bed? If a start has to be made to find out who positioned the cuddly toy on the bed three questions must be asked: who would have a reason, who had access to the bedroom and who had the opportunity to arrange the scene? In other words: means, motive and opportunity. Three very important questions because for whoever actually put Cuddlecat on the bed, the serious consequences will be inescapable. In fact there are only two possibilities: 1] The burglar did it. 2] Gerry or Kate did it. The first answer doesn't seem viable, for why would a [paedophile] burglar worry about a cuddly toy? Not only that, for this scenario doesn't explain the cadaver odour. For surely Madeleine was alive when she was abducted? Or did the burglar abduct a dead Madeleine? Nothing is impossible, but it is highly unlikely that he would have done anything like that. The second answer isn't so unlikely. Gerry and Kate had unlimited access to her room, bed and cuddly toy. They were the last people in the apartment that evening before the disappearance of Madeleine at 21.14h. Surely that would be a very good reason for any investigating officer to take 'a closer look' at the parents. For they certainly had access to the crime scene, a factor in the case that deserved closer scrutiny. If Scotland Yard still hasn't caught the burglar, it is quite possible that he simply doesn't exist. Would that be a possibility? Of course answer 2 appears to be the right one. Who else, apart from Gerry or Kate could have done it? Both of them had been in the apartment and had plenty of opportunity to put Cuddlecat on the bed. In order to prove that Madeleine had not left of her own free wil, as Kate was quick to point out. But thanks to Eddie the sniffer dog this claim is undeniably wrong. In fact it is quite the opposite, for we have the inexplicable fact that Madeleine's bed in which she lay asleep before she disappeared, **was not contaminated** with cadaver odour, whilst the cuddly toy on the same bed **was contaminated** with cadaver odour. This is not possible, somebody must have laid it on the bed **after** it had been contaminated by cadaver odour. **It cannot be otherwise**. It is in fact not important who actually did it, Gerry or Kate, but logically speaking it must have been one of the two. There can be no doubt whatsoever about that. It was Gerry or Kate who actually did it. End of discussion.

16. DAVID VS EDDIE

RECORD OF TAPE RECORDED INTERVIEW
Police Exhibit No IM24A
Person Interviewed: David PAYNE Date of Interview: 11.04.08
Time Commenced: 13:19 hours
Time Concluded: 14:59 hours
Duration of Interview: 100 minutes
Interviewing Officer(s): DC 1485 MESSIAH
Other Persons Present: None

David Payne, quote: 'So I walked back err from the tennis courts, err back to err you know Kate and Gerry's apartment and the time you know looking at, you know we've looked obviously at photographs since then and you know the time that we've got that I was you know going to Kate's about six thirty, err and I went into their apartment through the patio doors. The three children were all you know dressed you know in their pyjamas, you know they looked immaculate, you know they were just like angels, they all looked so happy and well looked after and content and I said to Kate, you know it's a bit early...' End quote.

The above is a quote from part of the interview of David Payne, recorded on the 11th of April 2008, which took place in England. Here he describes the moment on Thursday the 3rd of May, when he went to see Kate early in the evening, as Gerry had asked him to go and see if she needed any help with the children. Gerry was playing tennis at the time. So David went to apartment 5A which is the one Gerry and Kate occupied and enters the apartment via the patio doors into the living room where he finds Madeleine, Amelie and Sean, all wearing their pyjamas. He is quite carried away in his over-enthusiastic statement: 'They looked immaculate, you know they were just like angels, they all looked so happy and well looked after and content.' All that information in just one sentence, having been asked whether he saw Madeleine at that time. Such an answer feels rather forced. And of course the children could have looked immaculate; children who've just been bathed, had their hair combed and been dressed in clean white pyjamas, certainly one can say just that. And not only that, you could even say that they looked like 'little angels' but that should be more than enough. Mostly because the interviewer did not ask for these details. [David Payne could simply have answered 'Yes, Gerry asked me to have a look and Kate was getting them ready for bed]. But this is still not enough for David Payne; he continues to tell us that the children are very well cared for by Gerry and Kate. And also that they look so happy and content. A description so exaggerated, and moreover, unprompted, could mean that David Payne had a very good reason to describe the children as he did. Did he want to record in this subtle way that Madeleine was still alive at that time? It certainly looks like it. But he has, so to speak, shot himself in the foot. For the above statement given by him contradicts another very important 'statement', that is the evidence gathered by Eddie the CSI cadaver dog. To understand the importance of these dogs, here is a brief explanation of how they are trained and used. These dogs are also known as Enhanced Victim Recovery Dogs [EVRDs] and they have been specially trained to find dead bodies. They are used not only in criminal investigations but in cases such as the aftermath of disasters, collapsed buildings and so on, to find bodies buried in the rubble. Obviously the dog's nose is his means of tracking the scent of human cadaver, as his nose is many times more sensitive than a human nose, but he is also trained to exhibit a certain behaviour when he wants to let his handler know that he has found the scent which he has been trained to react to, disregarding all other scents. The dog will let his handler know that he has found the scent by either barking or by sitting quietly near the source of the scent, often this will be a corpse [or body parts]. These EVRDs are trained in tracking down 'wet' traces such as blood, bodily fluids or decomposing tissues. They are also trained to search for the bodies which are the 'source' of the cadaver scent and not just to stop at the scent without tracking the cadaver scent to its source [the corpse or body parts]. In 2007 Eddie was in the absolute top of the EVRDs; in more than 200 cases where his services were required this Spaniel obtained a 100% score. Eddie was especially flown over from the UK to Portugal, together with his own handler and a 'blood dog' named Keela. Keela is also a Spaniel and she too had an impeccable reputation for her score is also 100%. In the world of sniffer dogs these achievements are exceptional; other top dogs didn't come even close to these results. Both British dogs were very well known by all investigation services in the UK. So as far as results goes, these 'super' EVRDs, who also had a very experienced handler, named Martin Grime, are unparalleled. And no, Martin Grime isn't just some dog owner, considering his activities over the years; he had at the time some thirty-five years of experience training sniffer dogs. Apart from being a specialist in training these dogs he was also special advisor for the US Department of Justice [DoJ] and for the Federal Bureau of Investigation [FBI], with reference to their Canine Forensic Program. Apart from that, at the time of the disappearance of Madeleine he advised police services in the UK and abroad on the best use of sniffer dogs in cases of homicide. He was not only accredited by the Association of Police Chiefs in England and Wales, but he was also a qualified dog trainer and registered as an expert in that field by the British National Policing Improvement Agency [NPIA].

We now return to the investigation with Eddie the cadaver dog in the apartment of the McCanns, which took place some three months after the disappearance. Martin Grime reported that something very unusual happened which had virtually no precedent: Eddie ignored Grime's 'stay' command when he stood on the threshold of apartment 5A. Instead of obeying the command the dog went straight to the bedroom of the parents and gave the 'alert', in the far corner inside the large wardrobe...

Every human secretes VOC. It is a type of body odour which the human nose does not register but dogs detect it easily. VOC are Volatile Organic Compounds. These scents change the moment a person dies. Blood, for instance, will smell quite different than normal due to the lack of oxygen. The initial changes are minimal; although the decomposition process has already started but has not fully developed; quite a few organs and cells are still technically alive in the first few hours after death. Ed Kraszewski, spokesman and staff member of the Countrywide Unit of the National Police in the Netherlands, is of the opinion that dogs are able to detect these initial minimal differences of scent, as long as they have been trained to do so. But it isn't really the case that dogs are trained for this initial phase because they aren't usually deployed that early in a search. According to this spokesman it is certainly possible that a 'cadaver dog' will react to remnants of decomposing tissue, blood or body fluids some three months after the dead body has been in that place. [In Madeleine's case no tissue, blood or other body fluids were found in the wardrobe.] When asked what the capabilities of the Dutch EVRDs are, the spokesman gave an example of a successful deployment of a cadaver dog. The dog in question found two bodies which had been completely cemented inside the wall of a house. The wall was also tiled, even so the dog detected the scent of death. That is indeed an impressive result and a very good example of the 'power' of the nose of a dog.

The question which is very important, and at issue here, is as follows: for how long does a body have to be in a state of decomposition before it produces enough 'cadaver scent' [residue] which can be detected by a cadaver dog three months after the dead body had been there? We know from David Payne that he saw Madeleine at 18.30h. From Jane Tanner we know that she saw the abductor with Madeleine at 21.15h. According to these statements, it is clear that she has been dead in the apartment for at most two hours and forty-five minutes. From about 18.30h when David Payne saw all three children, until 21.15h when Jane saw the abductor with Madeleine. It is the only possible time frame.

Back to the question: how long does a body have to decompose before sufficient 'cadaver scent' [residue] is produced which can be detected by a cadaver dog, as much as three months after the cadaver has been in that location? Mrs. Esther van Neerbos of the Foundation Search and Rescue Dogs in North-Brabant in the Netherlands, gave this answer. "It does take some time, I don't know how long exactly, but in any case more than a few hours before the decomposition process is sufficiently advanced to leave a scent [residue] which can still be detected some three months later by a specially trained dog." She added that, as a rule, the Dutch police don't look for a body with a cadaver dog until three days have elapsed after the search started. Mrs. Van Neerbos is a leading member of this non-profit organisation, which has as its main aim to find missing persons and consequently to alleviate the pain and uncertainty of the remaining family and friends. The foundation has an excellent reputation and the dogs they work with have clocked up 8364 hours of searching and have found no less than 413 people. Apart from search actions in the Netherlands the foundation has also deployed their dogs in several international disaster zones, such as after the tsunami in Japan and the earthquake in the Phillipines. Consequently Mrs. Van Neerbos knows, considering her many years of experience, what she is talking about, that is clear. Dennis Janus, a dog handler with the Dutch National Police with many years of experience in these matters confirms what Mrs. Van Neerbos said. According to him too, the decomposing body doesn't leave a strong scent in a few hours. According to his expert opinion, a post-mortem interval of 2.5 to 3 hours must be maintained before a dog can smell the odour of a decomposing body. But in that case the body, blood or other body fluids must still be present in the location. The decomposition process is fully activated within 24 hours after the time of death, but in the early stages it is a slow process, he explained. He does add that certain factors can play a role in how fast the decomposition process develops, such as the temperature and the humidity of the surroundings. Yet another very experienced specialist in this field is Mrs. Adela Morris. She is the founder and CEO of the Institute for Canine Forensics [ICF], a non-profit organisation situated in the north of California, USA. Mrs. Morris has been involved with her dogs in numerous 'search and rescue' operations. She has trained her dogs specifically in 'human remains detection'. She organizes special training sessions, amongst others for the Sheriff's Office in Santa Clara county, for their Specialized Search Team [CSST]. She is a member of the Office of Emergency Services California/Task Force-3 and the NASA Disaster Assistance and Rescue Team [DART]. Apart from that she is also a member of the 'Bodie Foundation' and the 'Society for California Archaeology'. Adela Morris also does research into cadaver scent. She continually records how long it takes before a well-trained dog reacts to cadaver odour in different stages of the decomposition. She has also worked for the popular television series 'CSI: Crime Scene Investigation'. Taking all the above into account one may conclude that the expertise of Adela Morris regarding cadaver dogs cannot be doubted. After she was made aware of the situation concerning Madeleine McCann, she was very clear in her reply: "I'm not saying it's impossible that a dog doesn't obey a 'stay' command, but after three months there must have been either blood or the body must have lain long enough in that location to allow the decomposition to progress and to leave such a clear residue." She comments further: "I find it difficult to believe that a body stayed in a location for just a few hours and yet created such a strong residue which a dog is able to detect three months later." She is clear on this: "I'm not buying that." According to her expert opinion it is the case that if a dog ignores a 'stay' command and reacts so strongly to a cadaver scent residue, it means that the body must have been in that spot for several days, if not longer. Mrs. Morris emphasizes that she has done a lot of research and is still doing so in these cases. She has also concluded on the basis of years of research she did, that a post-mortem interval of 2.5 to 3 hours is the minimal time needed for a dog to scent a dead body. And here too: the body must be present in that location. The dog actually scents the dead body/tissue rather than the 'odour'. In Germany a scientific study was done in 2006 to determine the reliability of the so-called cadaver dogs. Although it wasn't the main aim of the study the researchers posed the 'most interesting question': for how long must a person be dead before the cadaver scent is detectable by specially trained dogs? The answer is no longer a surprise: the researchers are of the opinion that a post-mortem interval of 2 hours is 'a safe and demonstrable interval' to detect dead tissue. But the decomposing tissue, in fact the dead body, must still be present. [With Madeleine this was not the case as we know.] To this must be added that this extensive academic research took place under controlled conditions, therefore there may be some artificiality in the results. But all the same it confirms the statements from professionals in the field that given a post-mortem interval of 2.5 to 3 hours their dogs can find a body. As long as the dead body is still in that location. This research was done by the Institute of Legal Medicine, University Medical Centre Hamburg, Germany, Center Forensic Imaging and Virtopsy of the University of Bern, Switserland, State Police Academy [LPS36], Department of Internal Affairs, Hamburg, Germany and the Police Faculty, Technical College for Public Administration, Hamburg, Germany. The science-based character of this study gives no reason to doubt the conclusions of the researchers.

The 'statement' of Eddie the cadaver dog crushes Dr. David Payne's statement and leaves no room for discussion: he has told an untruth about the time when he last saw Madeleine alive. From an in-depth analysis of the results and taking into account the opinion of the experts, it therefore appears that it is forensically impossible for him to see Madeleine alive at 18.30h on Thursday evening. Certainly a strong statement but forensically this can easily be proved. A dead body simply needs far more 'decomposition time' before it will leave sufficient cadaver scent that can still be traced some three months later by a cadaver dog. It is clear that the dead body of Madeleine has lain there much longer, probably three, maybe four days, to produce a strong and lasting scent. And as it also takes about three days before the human nose will detect the cadaver odour, there can be only one explanation: Madeleine died much earlier than is generally believed [Thursday]. And we know all of this thanks to forensic science and the wet nose of Eddie the cadaver dog.

There is one question which will not be discussed further in this book but it certainly deserves some attention: why did the British dog handler Martin Grime never mention in his report that the corpse must have been left in the wardrobe rather longer than two hours and forty-five minutes? Because otherwise his dog would never have entered the parents' bedroom with such enthusiasm? Did he not know that a body really must have been in one location for rather more than a couple of hours to produce sufficient cadaver odour to enable a dog to detect the presence of death? As his colleagues know very well? Wasn't he aware of this forensic rule? Taking into account his extensive knowledge and experience in this field it seems very unlikely that he did not know this. The next question is: why didn't Martin Grime put this in his report? Was there a reason why he didn't mention any of this? Or did he really not know this? But as stated above, this book will not go into further detail, although the questions are certainly of interest.

17. "YES, OKAY."

If we assume that Gerry and Kate were involved in the disappearance of their daughter, we should also take a closer look at the holiday group as a whole to find out if it is likely that they were complicit in the 'abduction' of Madeleine. It is rather difficult to imagine that Gery and Kate created the scenario of abduction by a paedophile burglar all by themselves, moreover to have organised and performed all this without any of the group knowing about it. Realistically speaking that doesn't seem possible. But from the statements of the entire holiday group it appears to be plain that none of them 'knew' anything which could throw a light on the case. Apparently nobody noticed anything unusual in the way Gerry and Kate behaved, neither did they recall whether they had seen Madeleine on a certain day. As was extensively discussed in the book 'Madeleine: The Truth Is Out There', it is clear that the revealing statements given to the police by the Smith family from Ireland are of overriding importance. It is crucial to regard these statements, concerning their meeting in downtown Praia da Luz with the 'man with the child' on the night of the disappearance, as the perfect truth. It all fits together so well, two independent witnesses from the Tapas bar declared independently from each other that Gerry wasn't present in the restaurant that night between 21.30h and 22.00h. Those two statements fit perfectly with the time the Smiths said they saw Gerry; they saw him around 21.45h that evening, carrying a small blond girl on in his arms. Devastating information for Gerry. But not just for him. For the other members of the holiday group would therefore, if the evidence of the Smiths and the Tapas bar employees are to be believed, be revealed to be complicit in the 'abduction'. This being through their own actions, their apparent protectiveness regarding Kate and by failing to see what the consequences of their actions will be. This is particularly the case with Dr. Matthew Oldfield and Dr. Russell O'Brien. To fully understand this we have to return to the Thursday evening, the 3rd of May 2007, the evening Madeleine disappeared. It was around 21.30h when Kate rose from the table to do her check on the children. Matthew Oldfield was about to do the same for his child and suggested to Kate that he could also check her apartment to see if everything was fine. So Kate could stay at the table, he was going to check his own daughter in any case to see if all was quiet, so no trouble to do this extra check at all. Kate agreed and took her place at the table again. Meanwhile Russell got up for his check on his own children and together with Matthew he left the Tapas bar. These few lines seal the fate of both Dr. Matthew Oldfield and Dr. Russell O'Brien. However, this is only true if the Smiths statements and those of the two Tapas bar employees are accepted as believable. And why not? These witnesses had no agenda or reason to invent a story and their statements were given independently from each other and they fully corroborate each other. We have the following situation: Gerry wasn't at the table in the Tapas bar at 21.30h. In any case he is no longer there when Matthew Oldfield offers to do Kate's check for her. And what does Kate do? She agrees that Matthew Oldfield can enter their apartment 5A to see if all is quiet. And here it all goes wrong for Dr. Oldfield. For the moment that Kate accepts his offer his complicity with the disappearance is clear; he must have been aware of Madeleine's fate. For, as stated earlier, when Matthew Oldfield offers to do Kate's check, Gerry is already on his way with Madeleine, towards downtown Praia da Luz. Kate obviously knows this. Madeleine's bed is empty. A very good reason to keep everyone away from apartment 5A, wouldn't you say? Knowing this, would Kate have allowed Matthew to enter apartment 5A to check whether Madeleine, Amelie and Sean were sleeping and all was quiet? Whilst Kate would know very well that Madeleine was not in her bed? Would she have accepted the offer? Would she? So what could have happened? Well, something like this: Matthew, totally unaware of what's really going on, enters the children's bedroom and sees that Madeleine is not in bed. He would surely run back to the Tapas bar, trigger the alarm and tell the group what's happened. And then what?

For Gerry isn't there; he is still on his way with Madeleine. As indeed four members of the Smith family have stated. So what happens next? Would it not seem very strange that Madeleine and Gerry are both gone? And nobody knows where he is? In that case the 'abduction' would have gone wrong right at the start and Kate could not allow that to happen. So the question remains: would Kate have said 'yes okay' when Matthew offered to help? Knowing that he would discover that Madeleine was not in her bed? Whilst Gerry wasn't anywhere to be found? The answer to that can only be 'yes' if Matthew Oldfield already knew that Madeleine wasn't in her bed. Indeed, Kate could then accept his offer, for she need not fear that Matthew would raise the alarm if he didn't see Madeleine. And that is exactly what Kate did say: 'Yes okay'. So Matthew didn't raise the alarm and later on he produced a nonsensical story about not having entered the children's room which meant that he wasn't sure if Madeleine was still in her bed. Nonsense because this story is again lacking in logic and plain good sense; you stand on the threshold of a children's room where the three children of your friends are sleeping. Not your own, but other people's children. Would one not expect that you take a few steps into the room to make sure whether one of them has fallen out of bed or that they are not covered by the blankets? Or something like that? You are after all a doctor, it's normal to expect you to look whether the children are all right and haven't been sick or anything? Matthew didn't do any of these simple things. But the same holds true for Dr. Russell O'Brien. For by joining Matthew without Kate changing her mind about doing the check herself, means that he is in the same position as Matthew. For Kate wouldn't want to run the risk of Russell discovering that Madeleine isn't in her bed. [She can't know at that moment that Russell won't enter her apartment at all.] This makes it fairly certain that Dr. Russell O'Brien knew all about Madeleine's fate. Kate was sure that the men wouldn't trigger the alarm when they failed to see Madeleine in the apartment. That is why Kate said 'okay'. That is why she let both men go there, nothing would happen. The collusion of both men appears to be quite clear here, unless the Smiths and the Tapas bar employees are believed to be unreliable. But that's not all. For it's quite hard to believe, if not impossible, that Matthew and Russell would leave their partners unaware of what they knew. That is surely not likely, keeping in mind that they would have to carry this secret with them for the rest of their lives. One can therefore assume that it is highly likely that Jane Tanner and Rachel Oldfield were also aware of Madeleine's fate, simply because their partners would surely have told them. This means that apart from Gerry and Kate, at least four others of the group were aware of the facts. And that is very nearly the entire group. Only Dr. David Payne and Dr. Fiona Payne appear to have stayed on the sidelines and didn't have to check on their children as they had a baby alarm with them. Even so it is unlikely that they didn't know what was going on. David and Gerry were very good friends who knew each other from their times as students and they also knew each other through their profession; they worked in the same hospital in Leicester. Within the group of holidaymakers the relation between the McCanns and the Paynes is one of 'best friends'. Therefore it seems very unlikely that Gerry wouldn't take his best and longtime friend into his confidence and tell him what was going on. In fact this means that the entire holiday group was aware of Madeleine's fate and also that they knew what happened to her that Thursday evening in May 2007. But only if the testimony of the Smiths and the two 'Tapas witnesses' are accepted as being credible and reliable. No matter how incredible it sounds, in that case, taking into account what is discussed above, we are looking at a conspiracy; six doctors who have colluded to conceal the truth about the fate of an innocent little girl.

18. THE LAST TIME?

Witness statement of Fatima Maria Serafim da Silva Espada
2007.05.08
03-Processos Vol III Pages 675 to 678
PJ Mark Warner Cleaner 08 May 07

'She states that this took place on Sunday 29nd April, just before she finished her morning work shift [13.30h] as she had the afternoon off that day. At about 13.15h she went to help her mother, who was cleaning apartment 1 of the same block [5] situated on the first floor. She clearly remembers seeing the girl accompanied by her siblings and mother leave their apartment [5A] and walk to the stairs leading to the floor above. She was very close to them at a distance of about 1 metre, observing their movements for a few moments because she was charmed by them. Madeleine led the way with a plate [perhaps plastic] in her hand bearing a piece of bread.'

This statement is from the official Portuguese police files and the deponent is Fatima da Silva Espada, a cleaner at the 'Ocean Club'. She told the police that on Sunday she saw the entire McCann family all together, so that must include Madeleine. She remembered it well: 'She noted the type of shoes the children were wearing, tennis shoes, light in colour she thinks, which had little lights along the soles, which lit up each time they stepped on the ground.' Because she found it such a touching scene, as she said in her statement, she observed the children for a short while before she continued with her work. She was certain that she saw Madeleine that Sunday afternoon; without any doubt, she recognized her from the many photographs doing the rounds in Praia da Luz.

What is so special about this statement? Well, it looks very much as if this is the last independent witness who has seen Madeleine. Of course the nannies say that they have seen Madeleine all that week, whilst meanwhile it has become clear that Madeleine cannot have been alive during the whole of that week. Therefore the statements given by the 'nannies' cannot be depended on, and it is even possible that the nannies would have a very good reason to be 'economical' with the truth. It is quite something if you can see that Madeleine's name is in the attendance register whilst you have never checked whether it was actually Madeleine who had been checked in and out. Too careless? Too absent-minded? Not really engaged in your work? Serious matters if the management of the 'Ocean Club' would blame them for not doing their duty and it could also be a potential reason to terminate their contracts.

Back to Fatima da Silva Espada's statement. She said that she saw all the members of the McCann family on Sunday. But that was Sunday, four days before the disappearance. Did no-one else see Madeleine after that Sunday? [Excluding of course Gerry and Kate and their holiday friends.] A completely independent witness? The answer to this question is no; no statement to that effect can be found in the files. Apparently only the holiday friends have seen her from time to time during that week, whilst there isn't a single witness statement in the files from someone who remembers having seen Madeleine on Monday, Tuesday or Wednesday. And that is rather curious, to put it mildly. At the same time this should have alerted the police investigators: find a witness who has seen her after Sunday. Apparently no such person has been found, if there was a search for someone like that at all, for there's nothing about this lack of independent witnesses in the very extensive police files. Of course absence of evidence isn't proof, but at the very least it is an indication that perhaps early in that holiday week, as early as Monday, 'something' had happened. There is another good reason to think that 'something' had already happened on Monday. For as from Monday the holiday friends all have lunch in one apartment, all together and of course including the children. However, Gerry, Kate and the children are the only ones having lunch in their own apartment, not once did they join their friends at lunch that week. Surely a bit strange? What could be the reason for this solitude? Wouldn't it be nice to join the rest of the group for lunch just once? Especially with all the children together? That could be fun surely?

But no, not for the McCanns it appears. One can only guess what the reason might be: suppose Madeleine was no longer alive by noon Monday and if Gerry Kate, Sean and Amelie would have joined the holiday group, wouldn't all their friends' children ask: "Where is Madeleine?", or maybe "Why isn't Madeleine with you?" Or other such difficult questions. Of course that was a risk they could not afford to take, children, in their innocence, talking to all sorts of people about things which needed to be concealed from all but those they could trust. Clearly such a situation had to be avoided and by having lunch with Sean and Amelie in their own apartment, this problem was under control. It was the only way to make sure the children of the holiday group wouldn't notice Madeleine's absence. Of course this doesn't have to be the case, but it does seem very likely that this is the reason the McCanns had lunch only with their own children after Sunday. But the question remains: is Fatima da Silva Espada truly the last independent witness who saw Madeleine alive? The answer must be yes, for there are no other statements by independent and credible witnesses who saw her after Sunday. Then it follows that the next question is: had something already happened on Monday? Before lunch?

19. FRIENDS IN HIGH PLACES

Apart from a great many of public figures, for reasons at present unknown, a large number of prominent politicians have also concerned themselves with the disappearance of Madeleine McCann. Or at least have taken an interest in the investigation which by now has already lasted some twelve years. Below are statements and letters from three political VIP sources who have all actively and publicly supported the McCanns.

At the end of May 2007 Chancellor **Gordon Brown** had several telephone conversations with Gerry. He offered both parents 'his full support' in their efforts to find their four-year old daughter. A spokesman for the McCanns confirmed that telephone conversations had taken place between Gerry McCann and Chancellor Gordon Brown. Further details of these conversations were not made public. The conversations took place against the background of the Chancellor's earlier offer to help when he met and spoke to other members of the McCann family in the UK. The letter reproduced below is dated the 12th of May 2011 and is from the Prime Minister of the UK, at that time, David Cameron. It is addressed to the McCanns. The Prime Minister appears to suggest in this letter that he wants to considerably increase the effort by the UK police to find Madeleine. At the same time he praises the parents for their ceaseless efforts and their courageous search for the truth.

Dear Kate and Gerry,

Thank you for your heartfelt and moving letter. Your ordeal is every parent's worst nightmare and my heart goes out to you both. I simply cannot imagine the pain you must have experienced over these four agonising years, and the strength and determination you have both shown throughout is remarkable.

I am actually aware of the frustration you must feel as more time goes by and yet no news is forthcoming. We discussed this when we met, but I realize that a further eighteen months have gone by since then.

That you have been so courageous over all this time, and have not given up, speaks volumes.

I have asked the Home Secretary to look into what more the Government could do to help Madeleine. She will be writing to you today, setting out new action involving the Metropolitan Police Service which we hope will help boost efforts in the search for Madeleine.

I sincerely hope this fresh approach will provide the investigation with the new momentum that it needs. I know that everyone hopes and prays for a successful outcome, and our thoughts remain with you and your family. We will, of course, stay in close touch with you throughout.

Yours, **David Cameron**

As it happens, it was the present Prime Minister Theresa May who was Home Secretary at the time and who, on the 11th of May 2011, sent an open letter to 'The Sun' newspaper setting out the measures the Home Office would take regarding the search for Madeleine. Below the letter as published by 'The Sun'.

'Four years after she went missing, Madeleine McCann is still always in our thoughts. So I welcome 'The Sun's' role in making sure that her case is not forgotten. None of us can know what Madeleine's parents, Kate and Gerry, have been going through. We can scarcely imagine the pain they have had to suffer of the pressure they have been under.

We all want to see this beautiful little girl returned to her parents. That is why we have been doing everything we can behind the scenes in the search for Madeleine. Although it might not always be in the public eye, the British authorities have never given up on their work to find Madeleine.

Today I am pleased to announce that the Prime Minister and I have agreed with the Metropolitan Police Commissioner that the Met will now be using its particular expertise to review the case. The Met have skills, techniques and know-how which we hope can bring a new perspective to the case.

The Home Office will be providing the necessary financial support. Of course, the Metropolitan Police cannot promise that this work will lead to Madeleine being found. But it is right that we should do everything we can to help. It is my sincere hope that this new police involvement will bring closer the day that Madeleine comes home.'

Theresa May.

To have no less than three successive Prime Ministers supporting you when you're going through the darkest period of your life is nothing short of marvellous. No doubt the McCanns will have seen it as such and may also have seen this support as confirming the abduction scenario they maintained. Even so it is exceptional that a head of government publicly gives his opinion during an ongoing police investigation and also clearly aligns himself with the McCanns whilst it is not at all clear what actually happened and who is responsible for this mysterious crime. This puts these Prime Ministers in a risky and vulnerable position, for should it be proved that Gerry and Kate were involved in the disappearance of their daughter, it becomes clear that one's Prime Minister has been lied to and deceived by the parents and that will not go unnoticed. The solid political support which has comfortably sustained the McCanns all those years can then weigh heavily against them. Deception of three Prime Ministers surely cannot be without consequences? How very embarrassing must it be for Gordon Brown, David Cameron and Theresa May? Apart from that, there is the enormous figure of more than twelve million pound which the still continuing investigation has already cost the taxpayer by now. And if the parents were involved, they knew from the start that the search for their daughter and her abductor was a complete waste of funds. Money in fact which came from the tax payers, that is to say: money from a compassionate society who supported the parents, giving not just moral support, but also financial help amounting to several million pounds, to enable them to continue the search for Madeleine. What could happen is that the same people who so generously donated to what they thought was a good cause, will demand their money back if there is proof that the parents were involved in the disappearance. For not only would the McCanns have publicly deceived three Prime Ministers, but in fact the entire British nation. It's difficult to see how this could not have consequences. But all the above will only become a reality if it can be proved that Gerry and Kate were involved in the disappearance of their daughter.

20. When did Madeleine die?

In a previous chapter it became clear that Madeleine cannot have died on Thursday. Immediately the big question presents itself: when did she die? A very important question for the earlier in the week this happened, the more time the McCanns would have had to organize 'something' to cover up her death and to invent the abduction scenario. To answer this question we have to look at the only available source of information, the official files of the investigation from the Portuguese Polícia Judiciária. Could something be found amongst the countless statements which could indicate which day she died? The first question to be answered is: when was Madeleine last seen by a credible independent witness? The answer is amazing. For it was Fatima da Silva Espada, a cleaner from the 'Ocean Club', who told the police that on Sunday April 29, around 13.15h, that is four days before the disappearance, she saw the whole McCann family together, so that included Madeleine. She recognized Madeleine from the photograph the McCanns later distributed throughout the resort. There are no credible independent witnesses to be found who have seen her at a later time than that Sunday afternoon. Naturally the entire Tapas group doesn't come under the heading of 'credible, independent witnesses' so none of their statements can be relied upon. The same goes for the 'nannies' at the crèche where Madeleine is said to have been that week. A critical analysis of the attendance records, which should show which children used the crèche, reveals that these records are not reliable; they are not complete and some entries appear to have been added at a later date. For example: Madeleine was taken to the crèche and signed in at 14.30h on Tuesday afternoon, but according to the records she was never signed out, as if someone had 'forgotten' to pick her up at the end of the afternoon. At least according to the attendance records, for there is no signature from whoever picked her up that day, which in turn means that, according to the administration of the crèche, she wasn't collected that afternoon. Not only that, but some signatures on the messy attendance register look very much like an amateurish effort to forge certain signatures. Apart from that the entries are incomplete. Moreover, no proof can be found that the nannies bothered to establish the identity of individual children, so whether it really was Madeleine who was taken to the crèche by either Kate or Gerry, or that it was a 'stand-in', remains an unanswered question. Just having Madeleine's name on a list isn't exactly foolproof evidence of her presence there. The attendance lists and the concurrent statements of the nannies can therefore not be taken as 100% reliable and therefore cannot be included in the search for the last 'moment of contact' with Madeleine and an independent witness. So if she was last seen by an independent witness on Sunday afternoon, one has to look at the following days; are there any details to be found in the investigation documents which could point to the possibility that Madeleine was no longer alive on Monday? As discussed in an earlier chapter [The last time?] after Sunday the McCanns no longer had lunch with the Tapas group; they were the only couple who had lunch in their own apartment for the rest of the week. The first day this took place was therefore Monday 30th April 2007. This is also the day that Madeleine is signed in at the crèche at 15.15h, but according to the attendance register Kate picks her up only fifteen minutes later at 15.30h. Just after fifteen minutes? What could have been the matter? Why was she picked up so quickly? Kate has never explained this, most likely because no-one ever asked her this question. But it could be important. Is this an indication that 'something' had gone wrong? The Vodafone records show that both Gerry and Kate had their mobiles switched off. Unlike the Saturday and Sunday, the first few days of the holiday. Why didn't they switch their mobiles on? Were they perhaps too busy with something else? Or didn't they feel up to answering any incoming calls? What could be the reason neither of them switched on their mobiles that Monday? And what was the pattern of mobile use on Tuesday the 1st May? The Vodafone records tell us that Gerry's phone is offline all day on Tuesday as it was on Monday. Kate however uses her mobile practically all day, starting early in the morning and staying online all day. In the evening between 22.15h and 22.30h she also sends off six sms messages. What else stands out on this Tuesday? [See chapter: 'Tuesday evening'] Of course this was the evening that one of the McCann children cried between 22.30h and 23.45h. But during that period the parents weren't in their apartment. Why did this have to be denied so strenuously by the McCanns? Apparently no-one was to know that there were 45 minutes 'unaccounted for', during which no-one knew where they were. No doubt they must have had a good reason to deny the evidence of their upstairs neighbour, but what reason might that be? For otherwise why so secretive about that timespan? But something else happens on Tuesday evening, at least something must have happened. For on Wednesday we find that one of the cots, in which either Sean or Amelie would sleep, has been moved to the parents' bedroom and is blocking access to the wardrobe. This is according to the statement of the cleaner who entered the apartment on the Wednesday morning to do her usual work. She is very sure in her statement, she has seen only one cot in each bedroom, full stop. It is not clear whether this cot was also in the parents' bedroom on the Monday night, because the cleaner wasn't on duty on Tuesday, so we have no witness statement about this event on that day. Therefore it is not clear whether the cot was moved there on Tuesday night or whether it had been moved there as early as Monday night. But we can be sure that the cot was there on Tuesday night. The cleaner knew exactly what she'd seen that Wednesday and the fact that the McCanns categorically denied this, seems to indicate that the bed was indeed in their bedroom. What follows are the inescapable questions: why was the cot moved to that room and why wasn't anyone allowed to know that? Once again, why should one be so secretive about a simple fact as the location of the cot? There could have been any number of reasons why the cot was moved to their bedroom. It could be that one of the children wasn't well, or that one of the children cried each night and kept the other children awake, or something like that? But no, the McCanns denied it categorically, there definitely had been no cot in their bedroom, the cleaner was mistaken and that was that. Nothing more from the McCanns about this episode. But why was the cot there? Is it possible that it was to act as an obstacle preventing the cleaner and/or the twins from getting to that part of the room? So that it wouldn't be easy to access or even open the wardrobe in which Madeleine's body was hidden? The same wardrobe that Eddie the cadaver dog alerted to? We don't know, but we may assume that the location of the cot is connected to whatever happened to Madeleine, for clearly it was a far too important point for the parents to let it go unchallenged. Although apparently the Polícia Judiciária seems to have let it go, the question of the cot came up again in the September 2007 interviews of both Gerry and Kate.

Gerry: 'It is not true that on a certain day they placed one crib in their room leaving the other in Madeleine's room' (Processo 10, pages 2567 to 2580, September 7/2007.) Kate: 'Regarding cleaning, this was provided by the complex on Mondays and Wednesdays. This was never modified, and it is not true that a crib was in her room or in a room other than Madeleine's.' (10-processo 2539-2551 6/09/07)

So clearly the placement of the cot was of considerable importance to the McCanns, even months later. It is a significant indication that as early as Tuesday events had to be improvised by the McCanns. One may conclude that 'something' had happened by then that required certain actions to be taken. It is likely that Madeleine died in the early days of that holiday week. Such as the McCanns mentioning Madeleine's name frequently in certain situations. It has already been discussed that the parents gave Madeleine a prominent role on the Thursday morning during breakfast. [See chapter: 'Why didn't you come?'] But there are more instances and one of these was on Thursday afternoon when Kate went jogging on the beach after her tennis lesson. She saw the whole Tapas group, minus her own family of course, and said at a later date that it was a shame she hadn't known the group was going to the beach that afternoon because Madeleine would have loved it. In this instance it is strange that she doesn't mention either Sean or Amelie but only Madeleine. Wouldn't they too have loved playing on the beach with the other children from the group? Why would it be only Madeleine who would have loved spending an afternoon on the beach and not Sean and Amelie too? It gets more puzzling when Fiona Payne later stated that she had in fact invited Kate to join them that afternoon, but she had booked a tennis lesson and it was therefore impossible to take the children to the beach. So Kate knew all about the beach party and it certainly seems that, once again, she distorts the truth in order to mention Madeleine's name. Then there is the night Kate slept in the 'children's room', on Wednesday night. She said that the reason was that Gerry hadn't paid her enough attention when the Tapas group was having drinks at the bar in the restaurant that night. So Kate was annoyed, at least that's what she said. According to her statement she was so cross with Gerry that she didn't walk home with him, but got to the apartment after Gerry arrived there. Once in the apartment she saw that Gerry was already in bed. She lay down beside him for a few minutes but he was already asleep. She then got up and went to the children's bedroom and went to sleep in the bed next to the window. The reason why she did this was because Gerry had ignored her when the group of friends was having a last drink at the bar, so it was a sort of revenge or punishment. But as she later said, she thought that Gerry hadn't even noticed that she hadn't slept next to him. A nice story, but does it ring true? Kate is apparently really annoyed with Gerry, but still lies next to him in bed for a bit? And only then does she go to another room to sleep with the children. And he doesn't even notice this because he's already asleep? But, as she said, she thought that Gerry hadn't even noticed that she'd left his side and had gone to the other room. It all sounds a little strange. For if you want to punish someone you must let him or her know what you're going to do in order for the person to be punished. Kate sleeping in another room had no effect on Gerry at all, simply because he didn't know. At least according to both their statements. Gerry also said the next morning that he thought Kate had gone to the other room because he was snoring, but he had not enquired further and Kate hadn't mentioned it either. It's clear that Kate's so-called 'revenge story' was nonsense. She needed an excuse to explain her presence in the children's room. For how else can one explain the actions Kate took 'out of revenge'? First she got into bed next to him, how annoyed can you be with your husband? Once again, another curious story is constructed, this time for the Wednesday night. Again, it just doesn't add up. What also stands out is the pattern of use of the mobiles, specifically on Wednesday 2nd of May. This is the case for both Gerry and Kate's phone. On that day Gerry receives no less than 14 sms messages from someone who has to this date not been identified. These sms messages are remarkable for two reasons. 1: Gerry doesn't even react to a single one of the messages and 2: at a later date he strongly denies receiving any of these texts. And Kate backs him up every time the subject comes up. Once again, a seemingly simple matter raises eyebrows one might say; apparently it was important for the McCanns to nip this story in the bud, so to speak, despite the fact that the mobile traffic was recorded by Vodafone. Perhaps the McCanns like to believe that the Vodafone computer network is independent of its users and can even conjure and register calls and sms messages out of the blue. Kate's use of her mobile gives rise to more questions; early on Wednesday morning at 07.36h she starts sending text messages, which does seem rather early. What had to be communicated so urgently in the early hours of the morning? It may have been something perfectly innocent but the time the sms was sent makes it stand out. For that is not all. As it happens it was also that Wednesday, the evening before the disappearance, that the Tapas group decides to stay out a little longer and have a few last drinks at the bar. Nothing strange about that, but because it is the evening before the disappearance and the first time they did this, it is worthy of note. Did they just want a last glass of wine or was there something to celebrate? Had they found a way out of the difficult situation they found themselves in? Had they found a solution for the McCanns' big problem, namely, where can we hide Madeleine? Is it possible that the 14 sms messages on Gerry's phone on that Wednesday afternoon had something to do with that? The fact that Gerry wiped all those messages off his phone does imply that certain information had to be kept secret. So what was it? What information had to be kept from the police? Another clear signal that suggests that Madeleine was no longer alive on Thursday and had died earlier that week comes from an interview of the parents by Antena 3, A Spanish TV station. The McCanns formulate their answers to the journalist in a way which is nothing short of revealing. What happened during that interview? After a short introduction to the viewers the journalist asks Kate: "Allow me to take you back to the 3rd of May. What is the last thing you remember of Madeleine?" A perfectly good question and it will be interesting to hear the answer. Kate: "Just a happy little girl. A beautiful happy little girl." Gerry cuts in here and says: "Just think of all the times... the nice times that we've had with her in our house and in her playing in the playroom with her... with her... the twins."

Dr. Martin Roberts, a British psychologist who had analyzed the case from an early date, published his incisive analysis of this interview with the McCanns as early as May 2009. It does seem that the simple question of the journalist took both the McCanns by surprise. Clearly they hadn't rehearsed this particular answer, for that is clear from the absurd answers given. Dr. Roberts wrote: 'Note that the question sought to elicit the last thing remembered, not a lasting remembrance. Gerry could not even place Madeleine in Portugal. He describes happy times at home in Leicester.' This is highly significant to put it mildly. What they should have said is crystal clear. Their last memory of Madeleine must be that she lay asleep in her bed, but that's all. For that must have been the case when they left the apartment to go to the Tapas restaurant? At least that is what both of them told the PJ: the children were asleep when they left. But for some reason the McCanns pretend that they do not understand the question and make crumbs of the expected answer. They could simply have said that the last memory of their daughter was of her asleep in bed, holding her Cuddlecat, but for some inexplicable reason they don't say that. The interviewer however, doesn't give up and formulates the same question in a different way, asking Kate again: 'Some questions concerning that night, 3rd of May, what's the last thing you remember of Madeleine that day?" The journalist can't make the question any clearer, he wants to know about the last memory on that [Thurs]day, there cannot be any doubt when it is put like this. And this is Kate's answer: "It's a little bit like as I mentioned before, she was very happy, errm…and very loving and, you know, I know Madeleine was very happy with her life. She's special." So once again she avoids answering the question. It only makes it more likely that Kate's last memory of Madeleine had to stay a secret. For at that moment she can't work out what her answer must be. And the reason she had to work it out is because she hasn't realized that Madeleine should indeed have been asleep in her bed. Her memory cannot help her recall the scene, because it simply isn't there to be recalled. But even though Kate didn't answer the question, she must have a last memory of her daughter. But it was probably not a memory she could share with the world. In any case, one can say it is very curious that neither of the parents had a last memory of their daughter on that fatal Thursday 3rd of May. Almost as if there was nothing to remember. Gerry realizes the danger and tries to say something about that Thursday. He tells the interviewer: "I saw her. I saw her and, errmm… I thought how beautiful she was and how lucky I was to be the father of three children." A lovely thought but at the same time somewhat strange. Father of three children? Possibly he wanted to stress that he had three children, but was unable to construct the sentence clearly. For he appears to have forgotten an adverb. He felt lucky because he was the father of three children. Not four or five, no three children. The sentence would have been far more logical if he'd say that he felt lucky because he was the father of three happy children or three beautiful children or possibly three sweet children, but no, Gerry sticks to being happy because he has three children. It seemed to be important to Gerry to stress that number and that fact, three children. He must have had a good reason to do so, but it is still a strange remark. His last memory of Madeleine was that he realized he was the lucky father of three children…

Almost five years later, when Gerry and Kate are in Sweden to do a television interview, the host of the show Fredrik Skavlan asks the same question as the journalist of Antena 3: "On May 3 2007, what's your strongest memory of Madeleine?" And this is how Gerry answered the question: "I think the strongest memory I have is of really, the photograph that was the last photograph [the fake pool photo] we have of her and err… you know, we'd had a lovely holiday. Madeleine was having a great time and just after lunch we went over to the pool area and, err… she was sitting there paddling in the pool and I was sitting next to her and she turned round and she's just beaming. And then the last time I saw her, which was probably minutes before she was taken, when she was lying asleep, and it's terrible how… I've said this a few times but I had one of those poignant moments as a parent where… I went into her room, and the door was open, and I… I just paused for a second and I looked, and she was sound asleep, and I thought how beautiful she was. The twins were asleep in the… in their cots and I thought how lucky we were. And within, you know, minutes that was shattered!" What becomes clear from this answer is that Gerry still, even after five years, is not able to come up with a believable story. Was there nothing funny to tell about her last dinner? Or maybe something that happened when they put the children to bed? Anything?

Despite all the factors mentioned in this chapter it is difficult to determine exactly when Madeleine died. The statement of the cleaner who told the PJ that she saw Madeleine on Sunday the 29th, together with her parents and her brother and sister is extremely important; this cleaner is almost certainly the last independent witness to have seen her. The following day, Monday 30th April, the McCanns do not use their mobiles at all and Madeleine appears to have been in the crèche for only fifteen minutes. There is no evidence that this was Madeleine, it could have been Russell's daughter Ella, who was about the same age and appearance. Getting Madeleine's name on the attendance list would have been 'evidence' that she was still alive on that Monday afternoon. Taking into account what is discussed in this chapter and in this book, the results of my own research and also information from the police investigation, it can be said that Madeleine died not earlier than Monday 30th April, but not later than Tuesday 1th of May. Within this time frame Madeleine probably died. It could have been as early as Monday morning, but it could also have been Monday night or Tuesday morning. But if you need one day, it is most likely that Madeleine died on Monday April 30 2007. This is clearly an important conclusion, for if this is the case it means that the McCanns had three days to find a solution for their problem and had time to carry out whatever was needed to achieve this. The solution which finally presented itself was a temporary hiding place where Madeleine would safely be hidden away from the world.

21. "GRANGE IS SIMPLY A WHITEWASH."

Not only those following the 'Madeleine story' were incensed about the way the investigation by Scotland Yard developed, as is crystal-clear when a retired Met police officer submits a formal complaint regarding the methods used by his ex-colleagues in their investigation, with the code name 'Operation Grange'. And he certainly doesn't beat around the bush as can be read below.

An open letter to 'Operation Grange' dated October 8th 2017 by John Coxon, former Met Police.

I wish to register a formal complaint in regard to 'Operation Grange', the so called Met Police search for Madeleine McCann. I do so on the following grounds.

1) It has blatantly and inexplicably failed to look at the parents and accompanying party as suspects in the investigation. This is in complete disregard to the findings in the original Portuguese investigation. Namely,

A) multiple and significant discrepancies in their accounts,

B) deletion of mobile phone data and obstruction of evidence,

C) multiple indications by forensic cadaver and blood dogs in their apartment on Kate McCann's clothing, the child's toy and on a vehicle they hired 3 weeks after her disappearance. Also a close DNA match found in the boot of the same vehicle.

D) An eye witness account naming Gerry McCann as the so called prime suspect, Smith man.

E) The McCanns refusal to cooperate, answer questions and take part in a reconstruction which shelved the original enquiry.

F) Allegations from two healthcare professionals that at least one of the party, doctor David Payne is a paedophile.

They were made suspects for all these perfectly valid reasons, it is apparent that 'Operation Grange' has failed to address a single one of them. The Portuguese closing report does not exonerate them at all, I presume during the 5 years of its existence 'Grange' was aware of these matters, yet has acted as if none of this ever happened. More specifically, Met police chief Hogan Howe has on at least one occasion claimed the McCanns have been 'ruled out', firstly this is at complete odds with Granges opening statement which claims 'treat the abduction as if it happened yesterday' clearly implying they were totally off the table from the start, secondly it is simply impossible as there is no independent evidence that exonerates them and if there was the McCanns publicity machine would be screaming it from the roof tops.

2) It is apparent lines of enquiry have been leaked to the media. If this were the case and a live child were being held captive, it would clearly endanger that individuals life, obviously a totally unacceptable situation. Furthermore these leaks have frequently coincided with an ongoing civil case the McCanns are fighting in Portugal, too frequently for comfort.

3) This failure to investigate properly has boosted the McCanns public profile, helped promote KMs book sales and enabled them to take on further projects. Do you believe, for instance KM would have been made an ambassador for a charity had the Met asked her the same 48 questions she refused to answer in Portugal? I doubt it.

4) Grange has wasted huge amounts of public money and police time chasing shadows in Portugal which its legal advisors must surely have told them were not viable lines of enquiry. In other words it has done a lot of work and spent a lot of money for the sake of doing it, no other credible reason.

The conclusions here are blatantly obvious. 'Operation Grange' is a whitewash, a vast PR exercise to promote an abduction scenario that not one shred of evidence exists to support ever even happened. The implications are equally obvious.

A) It obstructs the real police investigation going on in Portugal.

B) It potentially supports a criminal fraud of huge proportions the McCanns ongoing business.

C) It undermines the entire credibility of the whole Metropolitan Police Service [as if it needed any further help].

D) It threatens the credibility of the entire UK criminal justice system. In summary 'Grange' is simply corrupt, it has misappropriated huge amounts of public money, it potentially lets child murderers walk free, it is beyond a disgrace, it is worthy of extensive investigation in itself.

John Coxon, October 8th 2017.

22. Unusual patterns of behaviour

When a large police criminal investigation is launched it is the norm to construct a timeline of the day or days before the crime was committed. This is an excellent way to establish whether a suspect had the opportunity to commit the crime, in effect whether he or she had time to commit it. Moreover, such a timeline is an excellent method to reveal 'unusual behaviour' on the day in question. Were there events or did something occur which did not happen at other times? Changes in the normal routine of the day are seen as suspicious and are usually investigated further. In this way it quickly becomes clear which persons should be seen as suspects. A similar timeline is made for the behavioural patterns of the victim, the police tries to establish what the actions and movements of that person were in the period of time before the crime was committed and whether obvious changes can be seen in the normal lifestyle of the victim. A suspect who normally drives about sixty miles a day to commute to his work and back, will have to do some explaining if he suddenly changes this pattern and covers more than three hundred miles in one day. He may of course have a plausible explanation, but the question only arises if one has a clear insight in the normal and actual pattern. A timeline is the perfect method and many crimes have been solved because suspects could be confronted and asked to explain exceptional changes in their daily routine. It is therefore of some importance to find out whether in the Madeleine McCann case changes were made in the daily holiday routine. The so-called 'unusual patterns'.

Thursday 3rd May 2007

- For the first time that week Kate woke up in the children's bedroom.
- Madeleine asks her parents for the first and only time that week why they didn't come when she was crying?

- For the first time that week David and Fiona return already at 11.30h from the beach.
- For the first time that week the entire 'Tapas group' gathers around the swimming pool.
- For the first time that week Gerry has his mobile with him when he is at the swimming pool.
- For the first time that week Kate and Fiona collect their children from the crèche together.
- For the first time each couple from the Tapas group choose to have lunch in their own respective apartments.
- For the first time that week David, Matthew, Russell and Gerry organized a 'men's social'.
- Russell and Matthew go sailing on a catamaran for the first time.
- Gerry and Kate have a tennis lesson together for the first time that week.
- The Tapas group [apart from the McCanns] are all together on the beach for the first time.
- Madeleine, Sean and Amelie don't visit the play area after their supper for the first time that week.
- For the first time Matthew offers to do the 'children's check' for other members of the group.
- Matthew enters the apartment of Gerry and Kate for the first time on his own.
- Russell and Jane are looking after their sick daughter and for the first time take turns to look after her.
- For the first time that week a little girl disappeared from her bed...
  [Source: PJ files]

It is difficult to clearly assess the importance of the above, but what is very clear is that a lot of things were done differently for the first time on that dramatic day. In particular the fact that everybody had lunch in their own apartment that afternoon gives rise to a number of questions: why was this done? Was there any special reason to do so?

From the statements given by the group it is not clear why they all changed their normal routine, so it remains an interesting question. Until that Thursday the group had lunch all together in one apartment, except for Gerry and Kate who had lunch in their own apartment together with their children and who didn't even once join their fellow holidaymakers after Sunday for a get-together lunch with their friends.

23. LOOSE ENDS…

"What time is it?"

A witness whose testimony could have done with further investigation and who should have a second interview is Maria Manuela da Silva. That Thursday night, May 3rd 2007, she is the last known person to pass the McCann's apartment before Kate raised the alarm around 22.10h and she did notice something, as noted in her statement on the 8th of May 2007. For this witness knows the exact time when she and her boyfriend walked to their car, because she asked her friend what time it was. It was 21.58h. Barely a minute later they drove past the McCann's apartment. The witness stated that she looked at apartment 5A and at the one above that, [Mrs. Fenn's residence] and saw there were lights on, but she could not say for sure exactly where. Quote: 'States that she looked at the exit of the apartment and that from the flat above the McCanns, she saw light [..] but she could not define concretely where she saw the light when she passed the McCann apartment.' End quote. From the statement of Mrs. Fenn it is clear that she was at home that Thursday evening, and it is also known that she normally didn't go to bed early, so one may assume that the light this witness saw was in Mrs. Fenn's apartment. And that appears to be right, for by 21.59h, as we know, Kate isn't in the apartment yet; it's around that time that she gets up from the table in the Tapas bar to do her check on the children. At more or less the same moment this witness passed the apartment in a car and states that she has not seen anything unusual near the McCann's apartment. She did however notice a car which was parked close to the window of the apartment. At first sight this doesn't seem to be a very useful statement, but in fact it is. Not however, because of the car parked close by. This witness tells much more than she thinks, but unfortunately this escaped the detectives of the PJ at the time. For she tells that the car was parked close to the window of apartment 5A. That means that the car did not block the view of the window. No, for in that case the witness would have said that there was a car *in front* of the window. By including the window in her observation she wanted to point out the location of the car, but this means that clearly she must have observed the window, relative to the position of the car. The window behind which the three children of the McCann's lay asleep. Nothing else of interest was seen by Manuela as she told the police. And that is very strange, since by then Madeleine had been abducted some time ago and the window would have been open. As the distance between the witness and the window would have been no more than a few metres, it is not likely that she would have missed the open window. Don't forget that she looked in that direction because of the car parked close to the window. It should be clear that this is a crucial statement for if this witness is completely convinced that she did not see an open window through which curtains were blowing in the wind, or that she would have noticed if that had been the case, where does that lead to? Quote: 'States that she looked at the exit of the apartment] [..] nothing struck her as abnormal in that zone that would have raised her suspicions.' End quote. Surely this should have registered with the detective who interviewed this witness. But it seems not, for if this witness is sure that all was normal then the whole burglar story falls apart. No burglar who lifted Madeleine from her bed around 21.15h, climbed out through the window and was then seen by Jane Tanner crossing the road at the top. No broken or even open shutters, no open window. Nothing out of the ordinary, this from a witness who is very familiar with these apartments. Had she been interviewed further she may well have said that she was sure the shutters were down and that the window was closed. For in her statement she says that she looked at the front door of 5A. The open window is right next to it and if she had been asked for more details and would have confirmed that the window was definitely closed, Kate and company would need to explain a few things. It is a pity that no further questions were asked, for Maria da Silva's statement is a crucial element in the case, but unfortunately her statement was not followed up. One could argue that Manuela da Silva's boyfriend, whose name isn't known, wasn't interviewed at all. He must have had an even better view of the apartment and would have looked at the window, as Manueal da Silva says in her statement that she pointed the car out to him. We don't know if he could confirm the closed shutters and the closed window, because he was never asked to give a statement. So there it is. This statement is crucial because Kate has said in her statement that the shutters and the window were wide open when she entered the room. [Logical, for what else could she say?] But the timeline shows that witness Maria Manuela da Silva drove past the apartment at 22.00h and saw no opened window or raised shutters or indeed curtains blowing out in the breeze. Whereas Kate, who entered the apartment a few minutes later about 22.04h, did notice all of this. That is very strange, for the only one who has been in the apartment in that span of time is Kate herself. To check on the children as she told the police. It seems on balance logical that Kate herself rolled up the blinds and opened the window, for who else could have done it? That is the question, for just before Kate entered the apartment an independent witness saw no open window or raised shutters, something she certainly would have seen if this had been the case. It does appear to be sufficient reason to ask this witness to come back for further questioning and to find out what she might have seen and whether she looked at the window at all. This also goes for her boyfriend who was driving the car. But unfortunately, we only have this single, short and simple statement. It does seem that once again, the investigation team let two probably important witnesses slip through the net.

"Please don't hurt Madeleine"

Yet another witness whom the police appeared to have little interest in is Carolyn Kish, a British citizen who at the time of the disappearance had been living in Portugal for some nine years. On 21st of November 2007 she gave a statement to the Portuguese police, concerning a curious encounter with Gerry McCann. This took place on the 7th of May 2007, the fourth day after the disappearance of Madeleine, between 14.15h and 14.25h. Carolyn Kish needed to arrange a number of financial matters and for that reason she went to her bank in Lagos. On her way to the bank she saw and heard a man with a mobile telephone held to his ear and with a laptop under his arm. She told the police that she thought he was a journalist, mostly because of the laptop computer he was carrying. According to Carolyn the man was very agitated and was speaking loudly. This made her think he might be an actor, also because he kept repeating the same sentence: "Please don't hurt Madeleine, please don't hurt Madeleine." According to this witness the man also said something else which she couldn't understand. Carolyn said that there was nobody else around and that the man was initially about ten metres away from her, but once she got to the cashpoint he passed close behind her at about one metre distance. This enabled her to see the man very clearly and eventually, when Carolyn sees photographs broadcast on television, she identifies him as Gerry McCann. The obvious question is: who was Gerry talking to so furiously that Monday afternoon 7th of May 2007 in Lagos? The words 'please don't hurt Madeleine' suggested without doubt that whoever he was talking to had Madeleine in his power and could obviously be the abductor. Why else would Gerry plead not to hurt Madeleine? Surely no-one else? So that means that Gerry was contacted by the possible abductor. If that is the case why hasn't this been investigated? The first tangible sign that there was indeed an abductor at all? And why didn't Gerry report this to the police? At that time, the fourth day after the 'abduction', they could certainly use some concrete information about an abductor. They could have traced the phone call for a start, in 2007 this had been possible for many years and the call could have been traced to an individual and a location. But nothing concerning such an action can be found in the files of the Polícia Judiciára. Carolyn Kish's statement has however been filed and a copy was sent to their British colleagues. But nothing further happened. Surely it would have been very easy to trace the caller who spoke with Gerry that afternoon in Lagos. [How did the abductor obtain Gerry's phone number?] The telephone records requested from Vodafone give some startling information about this conversation. So startling that it is totally unbelievable that Gerry has never been questioned about this. For the telephone records tell clearly that this conversation never took place. It is not listed in the Vodafone records; Gerry's mobile hadn't been used that afternoon between 14.15h and 14.25h, so it is absolutely certain that this conversation never took place. Surely the investigators in Portugal must have discovered this as well? Wouldn't it have been a logical step to ask Gerry what this performance was all about? What was he doing that afternoon? And why did he speak so loudly that Carolyn Kish couldn't help but hear it? What was the object of this exercise? Did he, by giving such a performance, try to reinforce the abduction theory? Did he expect that Carolyn Kish would go to the police and give a statement about this incident? To tell them that Madeleine really must have been abducted because she had overheard the father pleading with the abductor for her safety? Wouldn't Gerry have realized that this conversation would not be found in the mobile data recorded by the Lagos mast? And that very likely questions might be asked why this was the case? The police investigators surely are curious to hear Gerry's explanation? But no, they didn't act on this information, although it is only fair to say that by the time Carolyn Kish gave her statement, the McCanns had already left Portugal. So far it doesn't seem likely that Scotland Yard has asked Gerry these very same questions. And that seems to be the end of that episode. Thanks, but no thanks Carolyn, they may have thought.

A pattern?

Gerry McCann should perhaps join an amateur theatre, for something happens on the evening of the disappearance which is rather curious. Just when the first excitement and confusion of the evening has gone, Gerry goes to the balcony with his mobile pressed to his ear. Apparently about to ring someone. According to a statement on December 6th 2007, given to the police by Graham McKenzie who was also a guest at the Ocean club, the following incident took place that evening at 23.00h: "OC guest G. McKenzie approached the McCann apartment from the bushes at the rear. Mr. McCann was absolutely distraught telling the person receiving the call that he feared 'she [Madeleine McCann] had been taken by paedophiles'. He said something along the lines of there being paedophile gangs in Portugal and that they had abducted Madeleine. I was so shocked by this, having originally thought that she had just wandered off." Anyone would fully understand that Mr. McKenzie was shocked when he heard this, for surely it isn't the first thing you think of when a child is found to be missing. In most cases a lost child will be found very quickly. Mr. McKenzie said that Gerry was 'absolutely distraught', which must mean that Gerry did his best to give a convincing performance. For that must be what it was, a performance, simply because he knew very well that Madeleine had not been abducted by a paedophile. So an interesting question would be who the recipient of the call was. To whom did he tell this 'paedophile story'? Again, here the Vodafone records provide the solution. Which is that neither of the two Praia da Luz masts registered a call from Gerry's mobile at or around that time. In other words: this telephone conversation never took place. Mr. McKenzie stated that Gerry didn't see him but he must be mistaken. Why? Because Gerry wouldn't have given his performance for there was nobody else near. No, it was intended that Mr. McKenzie heard the call and it is likely that Gerry saw him approach. Otherwise there was no reason for Gerry to perform this stage play, he knew perfectly well that Madeleine had not been taken away by a paedophile. Whichever way one looks at it, this conversation didn't take place. It would have been a valid reason to confront Gerry with these facts and ask him to explain himself. But in the following weeks no apparent action was taken to investigate this curious event. Gerry's play-acting shows how 'forensically aware' he was that evening, soon after Madeleine was found to be missing. A complete stranger is witness to a desperate father talking loudly about paedophiles. Perhaps Gerry hoped that this overheard 'conversation' would be passed on to the police. And that was exactly what happened. It only remains to point out that when he was noticed in Lagos by Carolyn Kish on the 7th May 2007, he did not have a conversation to the presumed abductor. That was yet another faked conversation conducted in a loud enough voice to be overheard. And as we now know the call that Mr. McKenzie overheard never took place either.

The real question is: what is the reason for this strange behaviour? Why the performance? The probable answer is that Gerry already, as from that evening, started to construct a smokescreen to tell all that there were paedophiles involved in the abduction. He did this most likely to distract the police and cause them to steer the investigation in the wrong direction. It would be interesting to know what Gerry would have answered if he had been asked to explain this staged performances. What would he have said? Or rather what could he have said? It's a pity these questions were never asked.

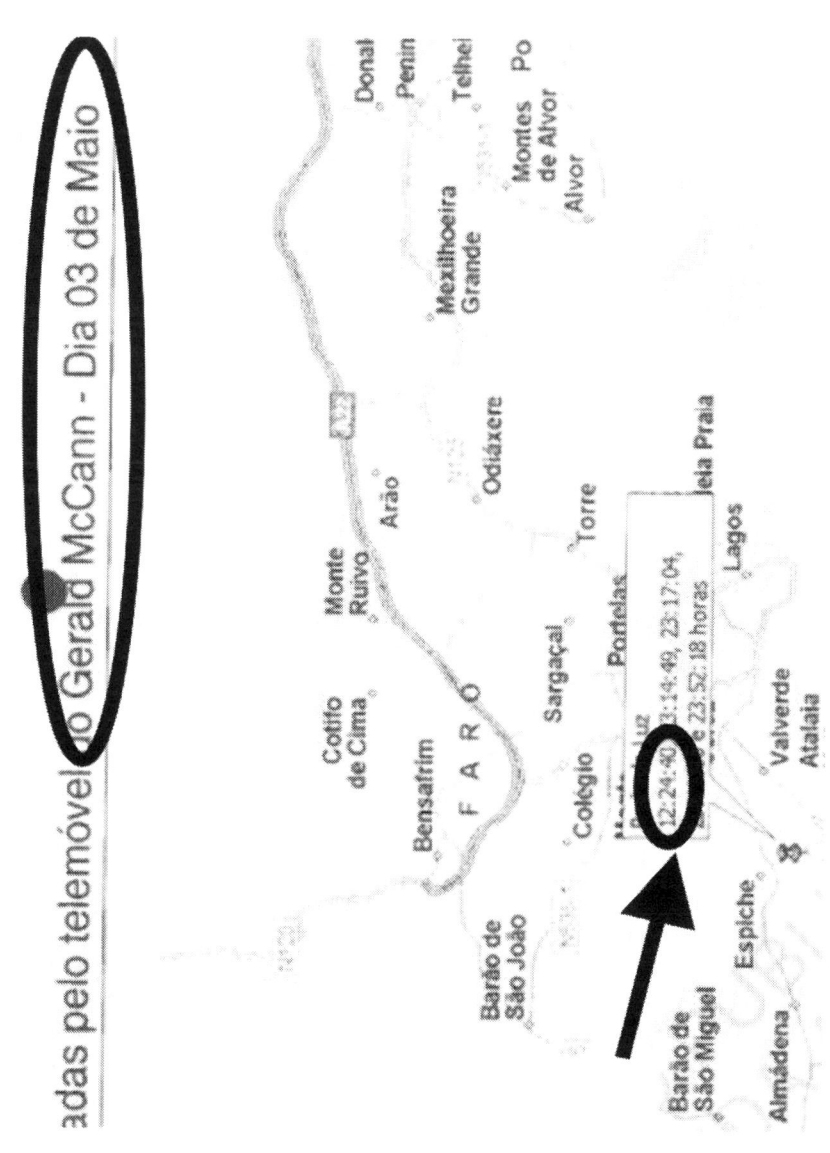

Source: PJ files

The mysterious 12-second phone call on Thursday at 12.24'40h.

2007-04-29 12:26:45	0447903108397	0447?206986188	Reino Unido	00:00:15	PRAIA DA LUZ CENTRO
2007-04-29 17:02:10	0447903108397				
2007-05-03 12:24:40	0447986651746	0447786986188	Reino Unido	00:00:12	PRAIA DA LUZ CENTRO
			Reino Unido	00:02:28	PRAIA DA LUZ CENTRO
2007-05-04 00:29:37	3510009627205 56	0447786986188	Optimus	00:04:53	PRAIA DA LUZ CENTRO
2007-05-04 00:38:40	0441854612157	0447786986188	Reino Unido	00:06:40	PRAIA DA LUZ CENTRO
2007-05-04 00:45:15	0441162302061	0447786986188	Reino Unido	00:01:18	PRAIA DA LUZ CENTRO
2007-05-04 00:47:41	3510009627205 56	0447786986188	Optimus	00:02:15	PRAIA DA LUZ CENTRO
2007-05-04 01:29:58	0441854612157	0447786986188	Reino Unido	00:03:36	PRAIA DA LUZ CENTRO
2007-05-04 01:43:55	0441416329874	0447786986188	Reino Unido	00:03:29	PRAIA DA LUZ CENTRO
2007-05-04 07:09:04	0447876791211	0447786986188	Reino Unido	00:03:26	PRAIA DA LUZ
2007-05-04 07:23:20	0447950627010	0447786986188	Reino Unido	00:05:53	PRAIA DA LUZ
2007-05-04 07:51:14	0441416329874	0447786986188	Reino Unido	00:01:26	PRAIA DA LUZ CENTRO
2007-05-04 09:01:55	0441162374055	0447786986188	Reino Unido	00:01:45	PRAIA DA LUZ
2007-05-04 09:04:16	0441416329874	0447786986188	Reino Unido	00:01:28	PRAIA DA LUZ

Column headers: Nº de Telefone Chamador · Localização da Chamada · Duração da Chamada

Source: Vodafone

The 12-second call in the Vodafone listing.

128

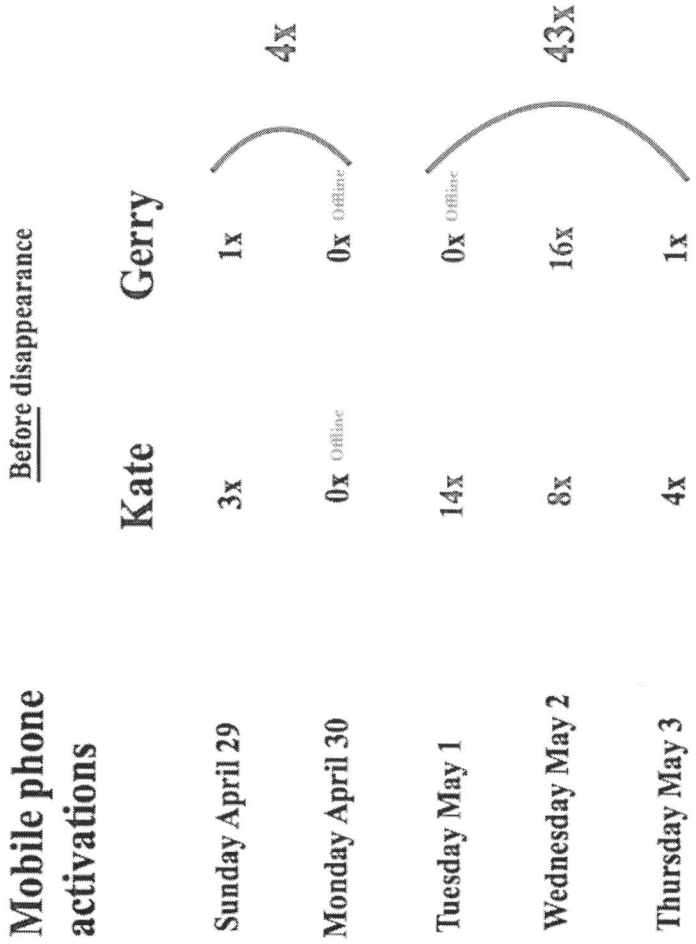

Source: PJ files   ©Peter Scharrenberg

The above table doesn't need much explanation. It's clear that the 'phone activities' of Gerry and Kate changed dramatically on Tuesday and Wednesday. Notice this is <u>before</u> the disappearance.

Source: Lobster's Attendance Form/Mark Warner

A good example of an attendance form of the 'Lobster' crèche, dated May 1st 2007. It's impossible to confirm the authenticity of all the signatures and the times that have been filled in. It looks messy, to say the least. A form like this leaves room for manipulation, therefore it cannot be taken seriously.

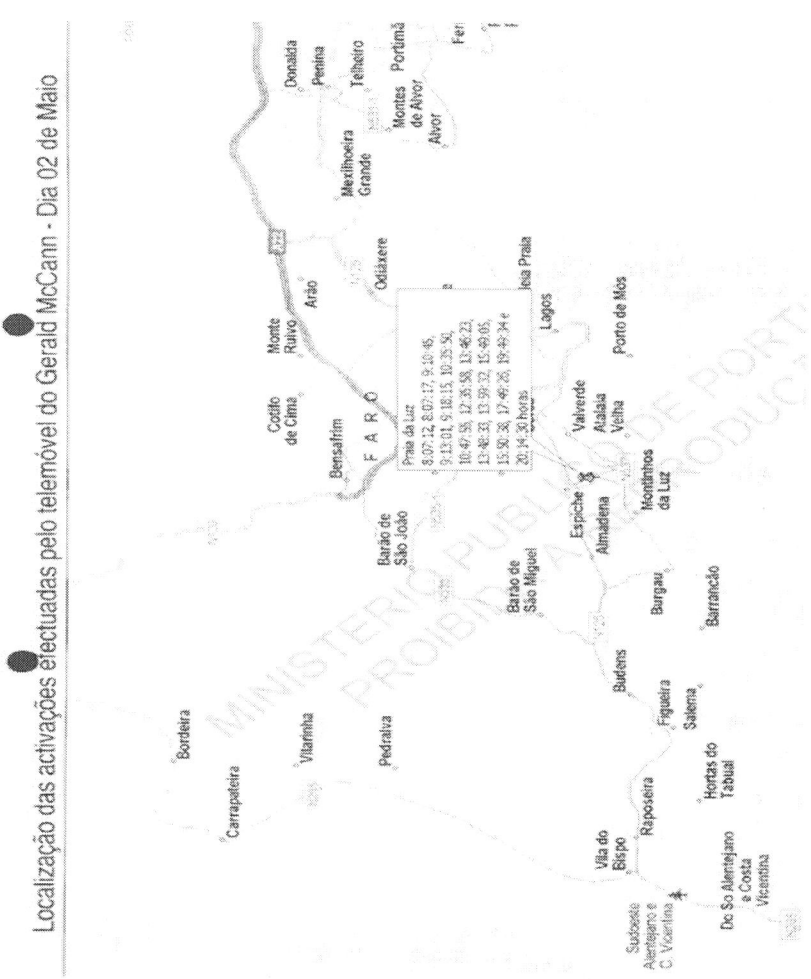

Localização das activações efectuadas pelo telemóvel do Gerald McCann · Dia 02 de Maio

Praia da Luz
8:07:12, 8:02:17, 9:10:45,
9:13:01, 9:18:15, 10:35:50,
10:47:58, 12:35:58, 13:46:23,
13:48:33, 13:59:32, 15:49:05,
15:50:36, 17:46:26, 19:49:34.e
20:14:30.horas

Source: PJ files

Fourteen text messages to Gerry's mobile phone on the day before the disappearance. It is unknown who sent these messages. It appears that Gerry doesn't react to one of them. He always said that he didn't receive these fourteen text messages.

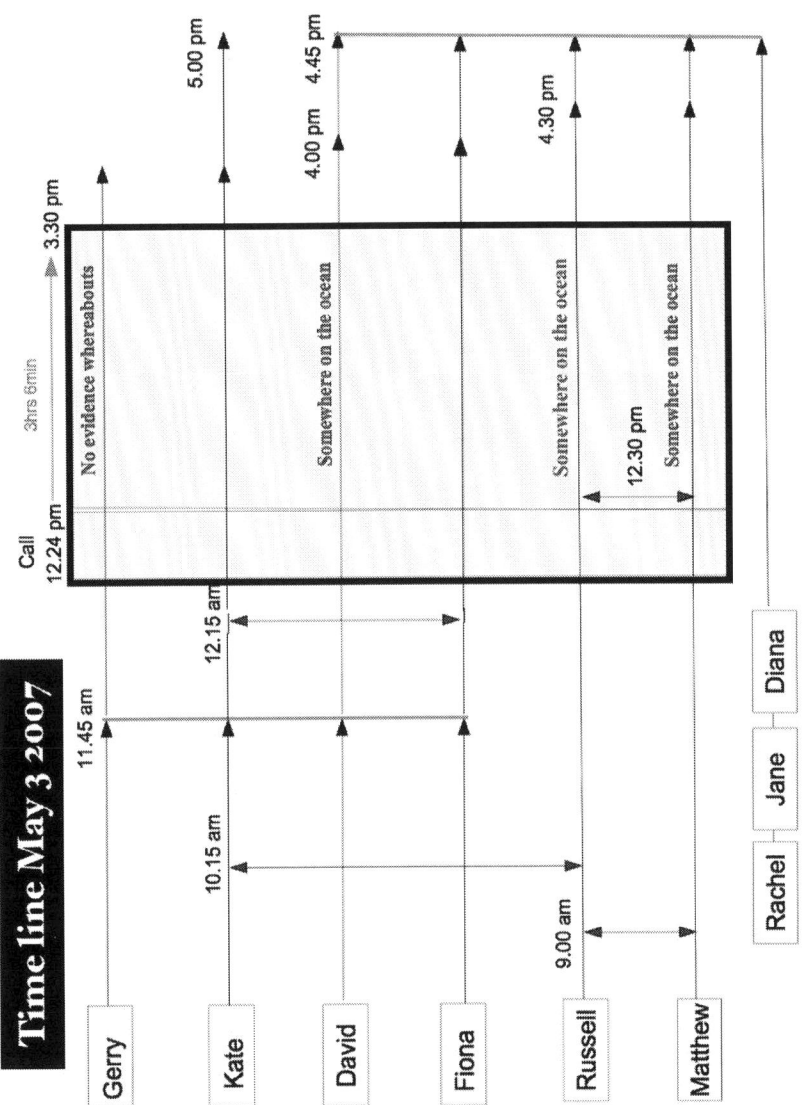

© Peter Scharrenberg

As clear as a time line can be: after the 12.24h call all the men disappear from the radar until around 15.30h. Nobody knows for sure if David Payne, Russell O'Brien and Matthew Oldfield did indeed go sailing that afternoon. And where was Gerry?

24. THE HILL, PART I

The ultimate aim of the police investigation is not only to determine who was or wasn't involved in the disappearance of Madeleine, but also to find her remains. Should this happen it would mean that Madeleine would finally get the beautiful funeral she deserves, surrounded by the people who loved her. She would have a grave that her brother Sean and sister Amelie can visit, to commemorate a sister they probably cannot remember. How sad. But it is of great importance that she is found, in order to say goodbye to her little soul with dignity, even after twelve years. And it will help those who loved her to remember an innocent little girl who had such a short time to live.

Follow the ~~money~~ cell phone

Without abandoning my journalistic objectivity I take as my starting point that Gerry and Kate McCann are responsible for the disappearance of Madeleine. That they had initially hidden her body and at a later date have given her a final resting place. This is the starting point of my investigation which struggles with that one question which needs an answer most of all: is there, within the information contained in the Polícia Judiciária files, a window of opportunity to be found which would have given Gerry and Kate the time to plan and arrange some kind of a funeral. And more than anything else: where could this have taken place? Not at all an easy question, but I have to try to find an answer.

It seems to me that the best and most obvious course of action is to thoroughly study Gerry and Kate's telephone records. Many pages with telephone numbers and other information covering a period of four months are waiting for me. I thought it was going to take a couple of days but it turned out to be two weeks of burning the midnight oil. But as I was going through the records I hoped that it would all be worth it in the end. The next phase of my research was to construct a timeline from the data of the telephone records, the calls, the text messages and pings. [A ping is a moment of contact between the nearest antenna and a mobile telephone. In order to alert the nearest antenna the telephone only needs to be switched on.] In the past many Mafiosi were caught because the police were tracking the flow of money from one location to another and in this way they could make a connection between one suspect and another. ['Follow the money' was the slogan]. These days tracking money has been replaced by sophisticated tracking of telephone traffic. Somebody who always carries his mobile with him, and who doesn't, can be followed in real-time by the pings his or her phone emit to the antennae it passes. But it is also possible to determine afterwards the route of a mobile phone, together of course with the owner of the device. So now I'm wondering if I can use this method to discover which areas were visited several times by Gerry and Kate. I know it won't be a simple task; the McCanns have more or less covered the Algarve in the four months they were there, at least if we consider the number of kilometres recorded on the odometer of their rental car. Nevertheless, this time-consuming job really needs to be done if I want to get an idea of their movements during those four months. Right now all I have are telephone numbers coupled to times and certain antennae. It is important to know where exactly the antennae are located and what area they cover. Every mast has its own number and name, often the name of the village or the area they cover. The records of calls and pings also show the times when a given mobile was used or alerted a specific antenna, leaving a record of the number called and the duration of the call, as well as placing the caller in a specific location. In the data pertaining to the mobile phone use of Gerry and Kate, I have records of in- and outgoing calls, in- and outgoing text messages and of the telephone pings from the antennae to their mobile phones when they enter its territory. So more than enough data to analyze. I'm curious to see where it will take me.

Indexing and analyzing the telephone records had already taken me a week and I'd got halfway without seeing any pattern which could give me an indication where this research was going. But I continued and hoped my perseverance would pay off eventually.

It seemed a good idea, just to take a break from the lists of numbers and symbols, to set down in black and white what exactly the McCanns' were looking for at that time, which was a suitable place to bury Madeleine. But what sort of conditions and location were they looking for? It's not exactly an easy task to find a place where you can bury someone without the risk of discovery. Obviously they would be looking for an area with a hundred precent privacy. Undoubtedly they would have asked themselves numerous questions like: are there any people around who can see us? Would we be noticed if we use this particular spot? Where do we park the car? Will it be noticed if we keep coming back to the same spot? And so on. Apparently they found a positive answer to all those questions for Madeleine has still not been found. [This suggests that the search is still going on, but that's not the case.] Even so, it is a good idea to list the conditions they were looking for: a quiet place where they would be able to dig a small grave and bury Madeleine. And it had to be a spot where they could return several times without anyone noticing their presence. Definitely not an easy task for the McCanns. This also explains why they clocked up so many kilometres in just a few months, from the furthest point west, Sagres, to Huelva in Spain in the east. The McCanns didn't seem to mind covering so much ground and it seems obvious why they did it at all: to find a suitable place to bury Madeleine. [This is probably the reason why they stayed in Portugal for so long; they needed to bury Madeleine.]

Back to my research. I've now spent two weeks on the time-consuming process and at last I have a clear overview of the mobile telephone data. Next I have to enter all the data, the calls, the pings and text messages, including the time and the masts which were used, on a detailed map of this part of Portugal, using little flags of different colours. I wondered if this method would work to discover where the McCanns could possibly have been able to prepare and carry out Madeleine's funeral. Will the map show me that they were several times in a certain area or even in a certain location? I'm looking at the pattern of flags on the map and realize that what I need is a filter to get rid of some of the chaos. First I remove the flags from all the antenna areas where they've not been pinged more than three times. So that means that all the areas where they've been pinged less than four times are removed from the map. Why four? I'll explain. Surely the McCanns must first have explored the area and not have taken action until they felt secure. But even when they don't do anything but look, they are pinged by the nearest antenna. [That is ping 1]. Next they have to find a spot where the ground will be suitable for digging a grave and finally they will have to dig that hole in the ground, it is not likely that this can be done during just one visit. So that means they will be in the same area for a second and third time [ping 2 and 3]. After these preparations they have to return to that area again for the body must be laid in the provisional grave and covered with earth and greenery [Ping 4]. I also feel that the McCanns would certainly want to return one last time to the grave, not only to check if everything was in order, but perhaps also to be near Madeleine for one last time. [Ping 5]. I feel that this applies more to Kate than Gerry, but I might be wrong. So: areas where Gerry and Kate haven't been more than three times do not qualify for this theory, because otherwise they would definitely been there more often. This means they would have been 'pinged' more frequently too. [Apart from in the larger towns such as Lagos, Portimão, Faro etc.] When I finally remove all the flags I no longer need something catches my eye. In one area there are quite a few flags which are all serviced by one antenna. I take another look, have I got it right? Next I check the Vodafone telephone records; did I stick the flags in the right spots or did I make a mistake? I check the call records carefully but can't find any discrepancy; the flags are in the right positions. I'm beginning to feel I'm on the right track. What I'm looking at is a pattern on the map with the little flags; this could well be 'something'. My journalistic nose scents the beginning of a trail. Could it be so obvious? Now I have to decide on the next step in this process. It seems best to translate all those flagged locations into days, times and antennae, but that has to be laid out neatly for those data will help create a timeline which will give a clear overview of the mobile telephone records. Including the recorded pings of Gerry and Kate's phones, and the times and their locations as recorded by the local mast. Once again I pick up the Vodafone records to make sure that the data I'm entering on my computer are listed accurately on the spreadsheet. Once I've done all that it becomes clear to me that my first impression of the data was correct. For here one can definitely see an area where the McCanns have been frequently and where they have spent some time, at least according to the call and ping records and those I trust implicitly. I decide to have a look on the ground so to speak, what sort of area it is and what one can do there. And how many people live around there and that sort of thing. I take my special map of this part of the country and find out how far the antenna Budens I covers the area I'm looking at. Budens is a small village not very far from Praia da Luz. The antenna for the village itself is Budens Parish and furthest away, west from the village of Budens, there is another antenna: Budens II. But I want to know which area is covered by Budens I, for according to the flags on my map this is the area the McCanns visited a lot of times. Five times to be precise, in the span of just seven days. And basically always near the end of the afternoon. They appear to have spent an hour to an hour and a half every time they went there. But as I noticed from the data, in the three preceding months they never went there once. What could this mean? I think visiting this area five times in seven days is quite a lot; giving me a good reason to focus on this particular spot. Google Maps gives me more information, it gives me an idea what the countryside near Budens is like. I can see immediately what could be the ideal place for Gerry and Kate; this is exactly the sort of area they were looking for. Still, now I have to find further information to support my provisional conclusion. This is getting very exciting, I grab a few other timelines which I'd made earlier and try to integrate that information with my latest timeline of the Budens I area. It's a bit of a puzzle but once I have entered all the data I can hardly believe my eyes. Now at last I'm sure, I'm on track as it were, the indications given in my timeline cannot all be due to coincidence. So would this be it? Would it be possible, for the first time and totally based on calls and ping records, to pinpoint an area which may be the last resting place of Madeleine? Only one question fills my head: is Madeleine buried there?

I have to explain this further: to start off with delineating the area covered by the antenna Budens I. In fact it is the case that the entire area south of the village of Budens, right up to the Atlantic coast, is covered by the Budens I antenna. Budens I covers the area between the mast Budens II in the west and mast Burgau I and II east of that area. The area covered by Budens I is, as I can see, uninhabited, boring, empty and nothing special. Should one not wish to be found, it would be a very good area to hide. Yes, there is something to be seen in the area, although it's not very exciting; just a few low walls, the remains of an old fortress left over from ancient times. Not exactly worth making a detour to see it. It isn't so much the 'attraction' of the modest ruin, as the parking area that has my interest. What? A parking area in the middle of nowhere? I get my notes out with my list of what the McCanns would have needed to bury Madeleine safely. Safe for them of course. I tick off the points on my list and read: 'a good place to park the car'. Well, this parking area appears to be a good place to park a car, so that's one important condition taken care of. A good place to park. Actually, this is the only suitable place to park a car for any length of time in the entire area that that is covered by Budens I. The road to the praia is narrow, a parked car would almost block the road. Parking frequently in that way would draw attention to them and that is exactly what Gerry and Kate didn't want to happen. Once again I look at the area on Google Maps and I now see that there is a fairly large hill close to the parking area. Bare and dry in some parts, but in other places there is a lot of vegetation, other parts are rocky. The hill is clearly uninhabited. From the parking area one can walk straight up the hill and after a ten minutes hike one is as good as invisible from the carpark. Is this the second condition fulfilled for their purpose? A quiet place, a lot of privacy, not overlooked by anyone in the vicinity and completely uninhabited? I check my list again, yes, that's quite possible. But I don't want to run before I can walk and so I now have to look for facts which may support this theory, for right now it is indeed no more than just a theory.

The timeline I've made was more than worth the time and effort, for it now gives me even more information. Far more. It tells me that Budens Parish, the mast that serves the village, has picked up Gerry's mobile on the 26th of July 2007 at 19.10h. [This does not mean that he was in the village at the time, for the surrounding area is also covered by the same mast.] Next the mast in Praia da Luz pings his mobile phone at 19.49h, without having been near enough to Budens I to alert that mast. Gerry is on the phone with somebody for practically the entire time during this round trip. It's unknown who was on the other side of that call. At first glance this doesn't have to be of much importance, but it certainly is. And here is why. On the 26th of July Gerry returned from an extended PR trip to Washington, USA. As there are no direct flights from the United States to Faro, Gerry had to make a stop-over. He probably returned via Frankfurt or Paris to Faro. Certainly a tiring journey for Gerry. First a flight from Washington [about seven hours], then two hours or so before he got a connection to Faro [about three hours]. When he finally arrives in Faro, it's still nearly an hour's drive to Praia da Luz. But that's not the end of it as far as Gerry is concerned. For after a short stop of a few minutes in Praia da Luz he's on his way again. [Kate has probably joined him there in the car.] Both are now on their way to the location I described above, to the Budens Parish area, for that is clear from the Vodafone records. He seems to have driven around there for a short while and then returned to Praia da Luz. This gives rise to a number of questions: what did Gerry have to do there that was so urgent? After such a tiring and long journey, couldn't it have waited until the next day? What was the pressing reason for this trip?

Is it possible that Gerry was in a panic? That is quite possible for just before Gerry boarded his return flight in Washington, he had heard that two sniffer dogs [Eddie and Keela] would be flown over from the UK to Portugal to help with the forensic investigations in Praia du Luz. That is according to my timeline. It does look as if he was shocked by this news, for otherwise this extra and apparently pointless trip to Budens Parish is hard to explain. It seems to be the prelude to what took place the following days. For that reason alone this mysterious trip is of interest, even though he never enters the area of Budens I. It is certainly noticeable that the expected arrival of the British sniffer dogs Eddie and Keela coincides with the connections the McCanns made in the area of the mast of Budens I. As the timeline shows, five visits in seven days to this desolate area seems to be too much of a good thing. And why, as my flags and lists have made clear, were the McCanns there every time in the late afternoon? What could they be doing there? In reality, very little. Even so, there must have been something there that the McCanns liked. But what? I now take yet another timeline and put it over the Budens I timeline I made earlier. And once again I see something remarkable appear in the new timeline. That 'something' is a remark made during a session of the civil court case which Gerry and Kate had started against the former Chief Inspector Gonçalo Amaral. They had decided to sue him because he had written a book about the case after he had resigned from the Polícia Judiciária. In this book he made it clear that the McCanns were strongly suspected of involvement in the disappearance of their daughter. During one of the court sessions in Lisbon Inspector Ricardo Paiva of the Polícia Judiciária stated that Kate had phoned him one evening. According to Inspector Paiva she was alone at that time; she was upset and was crying. "She said that she had a dream that Madeleine was on a hill and that we should search for her there", according to the Inspector. That telephone call took place in the last days of the month of July; Inspector Paiva couldn't say exactly which day it was, but it must have been one of the last days of the month of July, as he stated.

Once again, it is in the same period that both Gerry and Kate's mobile phones are pinged so often by the Budens I mast. The area with the hill. I wonder if it was this hill that was in Kate's dream. For during the period that she phoned the Inspector, she was in the Budens I area almost every day and therefore very near to the hill. Let's call it 'Kate's Hill' for the time being. Something else draws my attention. I see that on the 5th September 2007 the McCanns were in Salema. According to the telephone data they were definitely there at 15.12h and their mobiles were pinged in the same location at 18.38h. After that they are back in Praia da Luz at 19.14h. So it is safe to say that they've spent the best part of the afternoon in Salema. The question is, however, why Salema had suddenly become a place to visit. For in the previous four months they had not visited this village even once, but just a few days before they will leave Portugal to return to the Midlands, they suddenly decided to visit this village. What could have been the reason? It does seem a little strange. Why should you suddenly decide to go to there, and that just before you will be leaving Portugal? I must find an answer to that question, but how? And once again I pull up Google Maps and search for Salema, Portugal. Looking at the map on my screen I can hardly believe what I see. So that's where Salema is. Is that true? Yes, I've got it right, it's there, Salema. What's immediately obvious is the location of this tiny village. For it is situated right at the foot of the hill that we now know as 'Kate's Hill', but on the other side of it. So 'Kate's Hill' lies between the small ruins of an old fort and the parking area and the village of Salema. Again, this is quite striking, again an extended period of time spent very close to that hill, when they are nearing the end of their many months in Portugal. Surely this must mean something, but what? Could it be that they wanted to be near Madeleine's last resting place? For sentimental reasons? Did they hike to the top of the hill via Salema instead of via the parking area? To check the grave for a last time? It certainly looks like it, for why else should they suddenly visit Salema for the first time and so close to the date they left Portugal? And for so many hours. What did they do there? And why didn't Gerry mention this little excursion in his blog? Kate didn't write about it in her diary either. Neither do we find the visit to Salema mentioned in the book Kate wrote about the disappearance. So the obvious questions are: why not? Did they have something to hide? Was it important to keep this trip to Salema a secret? [And also the numerous visits to the Budens I area.] It certainly looks like it, for otherwise it is difficult to explain why the McCanns have never said or written anything about it. And again, that is not all. For it is on the 1st of August that Kate suddenly stops keeping her diary; it is true that the PJ took possession of her diary on the 31st July, but Kate didn't continue to write in another one. Might it have been a new phase, was there no longer any need to keep a diary? Madeleine was buried and did that mean that this was now another situation for Kate; was no longer keeping a diary a way to close a certain chapter in her life and a new beginning at the same time?

To summarise we can say that as from the 27th of July, Gerry and Kate's attention was suddenly focussed on the region covered by Budens I; no less than five visits to the site in seven days. And after that another three visits in August. But why? The area is largely uninhabited and certainly not attractive for hikers or beach lovers. It's main 'attraction' are a few low walls, some small ruins of an old fort and there's a fairly big hill. Not something one would want to see again, leave alone visit several times in such a short period. But the McCanns were there frequently for between an hour and an hour and a half and always in the late afternoon. One evening Gerry's mobile is also pinged by Budens I as late as 22.29h. This is strange, for during the day there's nothing of interest going on but at night and in the dark? For what reason would anyone want to drive to this area late at night? To do what? There are no streetlights in the area, not even in the parking area. And that's about all there is, so what was Gerry doing in that area? Considering the circumstances one might think that he had to do something which could not be done in the light of day. I wonder if this was the moment when Madeleine was put into her final resting place by her parents. A burial under cover of darkness? Is it the case that all the preparations were completed and it was time to bury her? The next day both Gerry and Kate are back in the same area, again in the late afternoon. It seems they found it hard to stay away. Or was it because they needed to see that whatever had been done in the dark would also remain hidden in the bright light of day? To see whether the burial in the dark had gone to plan and left no traces on the ground? So that, should anyone taking a walk on the hill, although I don't know why anybody would, he or she doesn't accidentally find a grave. I have no answer to all those questions and it is highly unlikely that we will ever know, for the only people who can say what happened there are Gerry and Kate themselves. But I feel that it is more than likely that something of the scenario I outlined above took place here; for we know that Madeleine must be buried somewhere, however and wherever that is. And that could very well be this hill in the Budens I area. For me this is the only credible location, taking into account all the telephone records, pings and other events during that span of time. It is therefore very likely that this hill became Madeleine's last resting place. A professionally conducted forensic search with cadaver dogs in that area will, in my opinion, lead to the discovery of Madeleine's remains. Because all the data fits a perfect and logical pattern leading to this conclusion. Madeleine is buried on the hill of Praia da Boca do Rio. And this was done on Wednesday evening of August 1st 2007, some time after 22.29h. By Gerry, most probably with Kate. But that's just a theory. Untill…

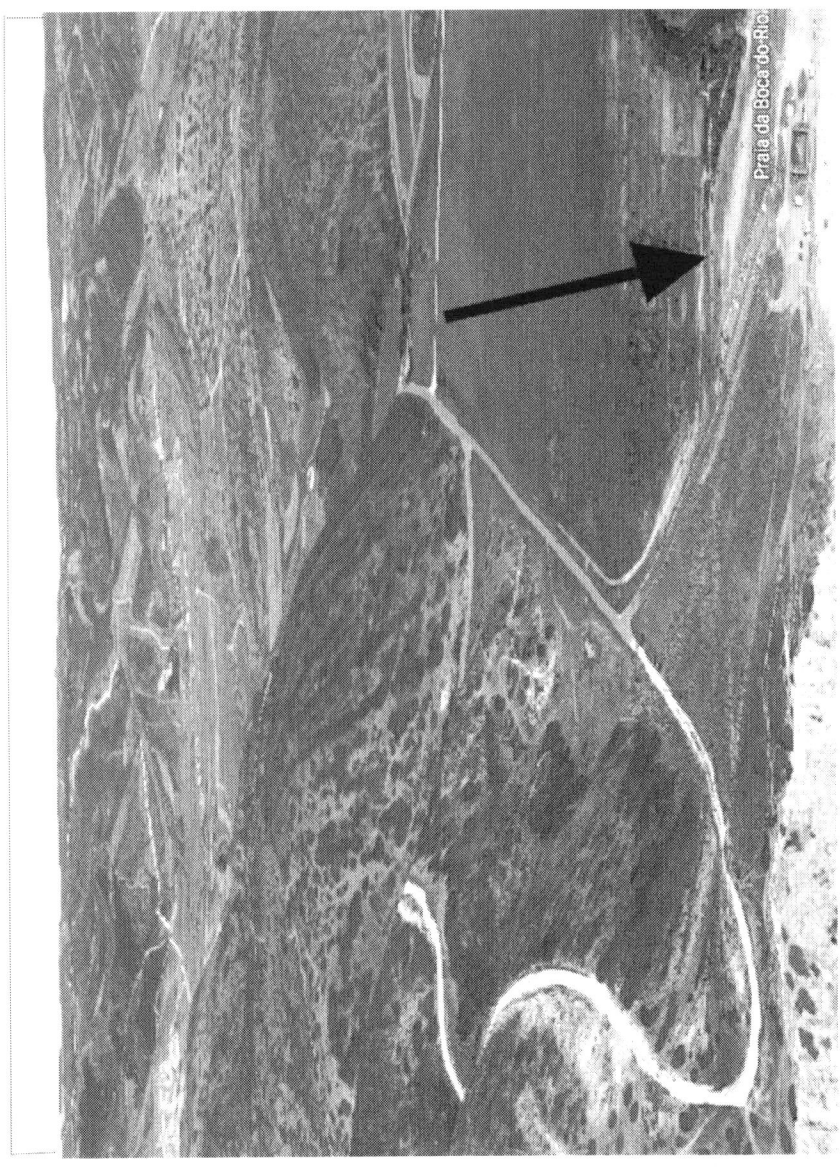

Source: Google Maps

It becomes clear from the picture above that the Budens I area is a very desolate place and there's not much to do. The arrow points to the parking area.

Source: Google Maps

How close of each other the parking area, the hill and the little village of Salema are becomes clear from this arial view. This picture is dated May 24, 2007. As can be seen, the larger parking area is not yet built.

Source: Google Maps

A view from the ocean side on the hill, the parking and Salema.
Is this hill the [temporarily?] resting place of Madeleine?

Photo: Peter Scharrenberg

After a short hike you're on the top of the hill. People at the carpark can't be seen from here. Which automatically means that when standing on the top you can't be seen by the people at the parking either.

Photo: Peter Scharrenberg

Another part of the hill with a lot of privacy. It's a very quiet
and deserted area and there's nothing to do.

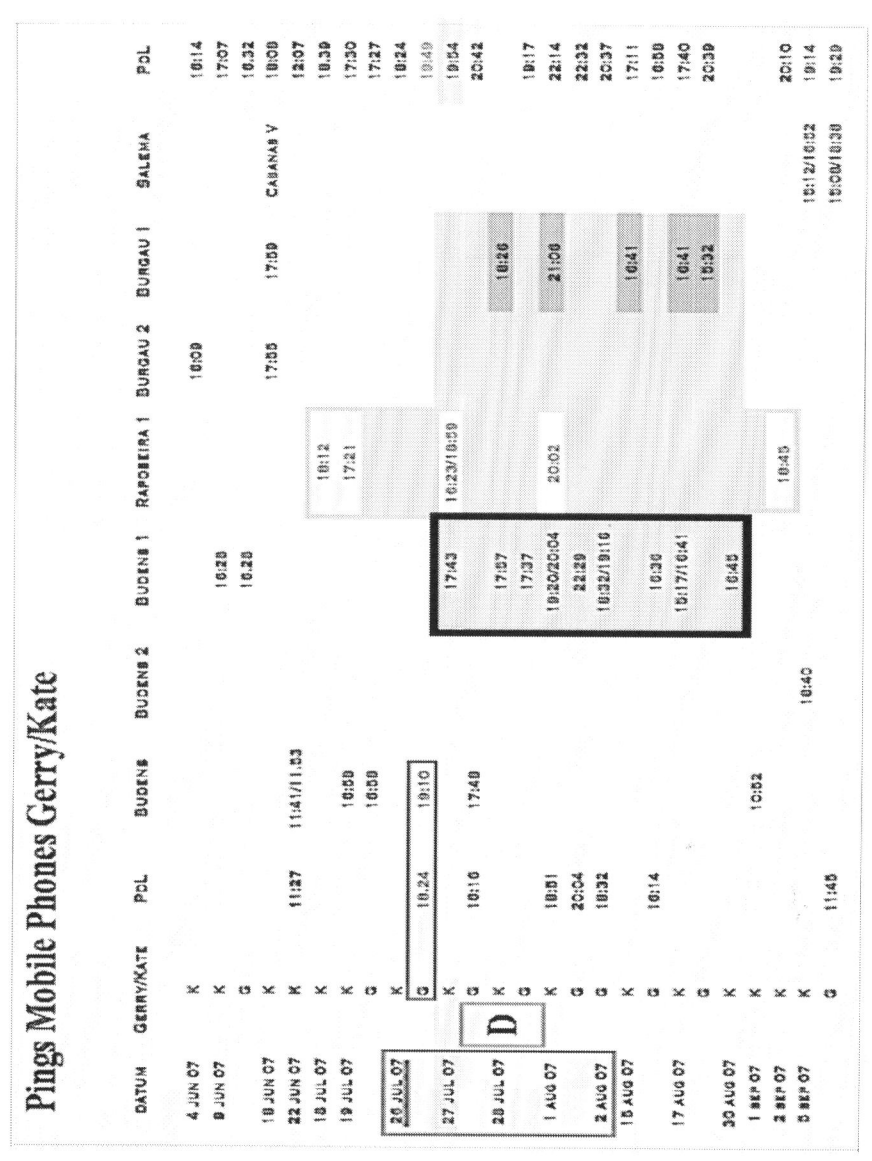

© Peter Scharrenberg

A timeline with pings of Gerry's and Kate's mobile. The numerous visits to the Budens I area, including the 22.29h visit, raise questions. What were they doing there?

Day 91 - 02/08/2007 | **Thursday**

DAY 91
OLD SITE
91-SCREENSHOT

Today was a bit of a write off for me as I was laid low with a probable viral illness which meant I could not stray too far from the house! I did manage to get through some e-mails, telephone calls and some paperwork. Feeling a bit better tonight so hopefully be back to normal tomorrow. Kate did manage to put up some of the new Madeleine posters in shops around Praia da Luz.. It is noticably busier, now that we are in August, with lots of tourists many of whom are from Portugal.

NEW SITE
91-SCREENSHOT

The figures from the National Center for Missing and Exploited Children show that one in six kids are recovered after being recognised from a poster.
Such statistics do encourage us that relatively simple measures may be effective in helping us find Madeleine.

Day 90 - 01/08/2007 | **Wednesday**

DAY 90
OLD SITE
90-SCREENSHOT

Another trip to the airport this morning to pick up our campaign manager. Kate did a series of interviews for womens magazines and the Sunday newspapers which took most of the afternoon. Kates

parents, who we visit regularly at home, also arrived and the twins

were very happy to see them. They will be staying with us for a week.

NEW SITE
90-SCREENSHOT

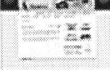

We have had some new posters designed of Madeleine, in Portuguese and Spanish, which I have been printing out to distribute locally.

I also did some filming to camera which we might use on the website and for future events.

Day 89 - 31/07/2007 | **Tuesday**

DAY 89
NEW SITE
69-SCREENSHOT

Relatively quiet day apart from phone calls and campaign related e-mails.

We have Busy couple of days coming up so off to bed relatively early (before midnight)!

Day 88 - 30/07/2007 | **Monday**

DAY 88
NEW SITE
68-SCREENSHOT

We had a routine meeting today with the Portuguese police. Kate and I are confident that every avenue is being explored and the vital piece of information that leads to Madeleine is only a phone call away.

Source: Gerry McCann's blog

As can be noticed from Gerry's blog, the numerous visits to the Budens I area are not shared with the world.

25. MR. Y.

During my extensive investigations in Praia da Luz, which involved quite a few 'off the record' conversations, I was given the name of a Portuguese man. As his name isn't important right now I will call him Mr. Y for the moment. Despite the fact that I was given plenty of 'useful tips' during my stay there ["Have a look at the cemetery" and "You have to go to the beach"], none of the information received was as clear as this suggestion. I cannot name the person who give me this tip, but I do consider him to be trustworthy. It's very unlikely that he would just give me this tip to make a good impression. But more than that I cannot say for I have promised him absolute anonymity. I will have to live with that for I know very well how sensitive the people in Praia da Luz still are, when anything regarding the disappearance of Madeleine McCann comes up in conversation. In short: they've had it with anything concerning the case. Starting up a new investigation of the case wouldn't be appreciated at all by the good citizens of Praia da Luz and my informant would not be very popular. But what he had to say is important, his name isn't. In any case this is a normal and useful journalistic method: promising anonymity to a important source; this makes it easier for informants to talk about potentially sensitive subjects. However, it still comes with a price. It means not only that the journalist has to search out sources that can be named, but he must also look for other facts which can corroborate or even prove that the anonymous information is the truth. One statement from one anonymous source, however credible it may appear to be, cannot be considered a fact. In other words, I had to prove that my informant knew what he was talking about. So that was my next job. I had to find out what the connection could be between Mr. Y and the disappearance of Madeleine. If there was one at all. I started my investigation into this person with just a name, Mr. Y, that's all I knew. But that situation changed soon enough as I discover that Mr. Y is connected to the medical profession, in fact he is a doctor, in Lisbon. I found an image of him on the internet; he has a friendly open expression on his face.

To protect his privacy that's all I'll say about his appearance. It did immediately strike me as a noteworthy coincidence; this was an interesting discovery. Mr. Y is a doctor, so from now on I will call him Dr. Y. That certainly fitted the profile of the Tapas group, with it's six doctors. Whichever way I look at it, this is a link with the Tapas group; they would have moved in the same 'circles', that is to say in 'medical circles'. The doctors in the Tapas group in the UK and Dr. Y in Portugal. I did realize that the UK and Portugal are rather far apart, but I had only just started my research on this doctor and all sorts of information could come up. A bit further on in my searches I found that Dr. Y is or was a member of a British Medical Association named [REDACTED.......] Unfortunately I couldn't find out when he was a member of this group, or indeed why, but it was certainly of interest that this Portuguese doctor was a member of this British association. My next discovery was a very big surprise. Because none other than Kate McCann was also an active member of this British organisation [REDACTED.......]. In particular in the years 20[..] and in 20[..] Information before this time is hard to find, possibly because of the change of name of the organisation. Finding Kate McCann's name on the members list of this organisation was quite a big surprise, although I think it's not necessarily the case that Kate knew Dr. Y through [REDACTED.....], it's still an interesting fact. Most probably Dr. Y was already active in the association at a earlier date than Kate. But it is still important, for it shows that they moved in the same British medical and academic world. I was beginning to get enthusiastic for this was a very clear link with the Tapas group and even with Kate. What else can I discover? Can I still find a direct link to the doctor with the Tapas group or possibly with the UK? The answer is 'yes'. Because I discovered that Dr. Y had also worked with the **UK Government** on programmes to promote health. I can hardly believe what I'm reading. He worked with the UK Government? This Portuguese doctor? A thought occurred to me, would he have lived in the UK at any time? When he worked for the UK Government? Considering the long-term projects he was involved in it doesn't seem too easy to manage all this work from Portugal. So it is quite possible that at one period in his career he lived and worked in the UK. Yes, that is certainly possible and quite logical in a way. And if this is indeed the case, the gap between the medical world of Dr. Y in Portugal and that of the doctors of the Tapas group in the UK is considerably less.

I search further to find an answer to the question: is there anything to be found to establish whether this doctor has lived in the UK? If so, that would mean that the chance is quite high that he met one of the doctors of the Tapas group in meetings or conferences of the British medical and academic world. But I'm also thinking of Professor X. [Chapter The 12-second call.] He too is a doctor. Can I find a link between Dr. Y and Professor X? Perhaps their academic careers have crossed at one time. Or is it possible they knew each other socially, were even friends perhaps. These are important questions which need to be answered.

Meanwhile I'm finding more and more British connections of Dr. Y. I read that he was a guest lecturer at a famous **British** university; this Portuguese doctor is beginning to show up more and more British connections. Next I find a comment by him in the **British** Medical Journal. This comment makes it clear that he was living in the UK when it was submitted. It is exactly what I was looking for, confirmation that Dr. Y did indeed live in the UK. The comment in the BMJ was published at the end of 20[..], which gave me a rough idea of the period he spent in the UK. I still find more information, for the doctor's name appears in an short article on a Portuguese website where he is mentioned as follows: '... for this reason, he graduated in **Reading, UK**, always sharing this dedication with […] Dr. Y, [...] with whom he went on counselling and exchanging ideas.' Surely that must be a British colleague who wrote these lines? Again that implies that Dr. Y lived in the UK for some time. And that means that he didn't just live in the same country as the doctors of the Tapas group, but also that he moved in the same circles, namely that of the British medical and academic establishment. Without any exaggeration it can be said that this Portuguese doctor has strong ties to the medical and academic world in the UK. Whichever way I look at it, it is a very clear link with the doctors of the Tapas group and with their social contacts, as well as their professions. I feel this is quite a discovery but I'm stuck with the information that this doctor lives and works in Lisbon; it wasn't at all clear how he could have helped the McCanns, for Lisbon is about 200 miles from Praia da Luz. So what could he have done for his colleagues when they were in a critical situation? It seemed to me that I could only answer that question by first considering what sort of help the McCanns needed at the time. Perhaps starting from that point I would find out how Dr. Y fitted into the whole picture. If he had a place in the affair at all, for that is not at all certain. But going through the results of my investigation so far it looked like a promising lead. So what did the McCanns need? That wasn't too difficult to determine: what they needed was a place to temporarily hide Madeleine's body. Somewhere completely out of sight, somewhere she would certainly not be found during the expected searches for her. That is in fact what they needed so urgently that night. But Dr. Y was in Lisbon hundreds of miles away. That could mean that this doctor wouldn't have been able to help Gerry and Kate, certainly not with a location to hide Madeleine for an indeterminate period of time. Unless, I suddenly realize... unless this doctor has a holiday home somewhere in the Algarve. I know that many well-to-do Portuguese own holiday homes to escape the heat of the capital Lisbon in the summer months. Would the doctor be one of these and would he have a holiday home the Algarve? It was a long shot, but not a unreasonable one, and I decided to follow it up. I needed to find out if he did own a property there. I phoned a contact I have in Portugal and asked him if he would be able to find out from the appropriate authorities, or otherwise, whether Dr. Y owns a house or villa in the Algarve or even in Praia da Luz itself. Surely such information must be available somewhere. If he did or does own a house there it would be quite a discovery; such a 'British' Portuguese doctor having a holiday home in Praia da Luz. But for now it's nothing but a thought. When my Portuguese contact phones back some six hours later with the result of his search, another puzzle piece slots into its place. Not totally unexpected but I was surprised anyway: Dr. Y did indeed own a holiday home in the Algarve. And not only that, it was located in Praia da Luz. My initial guess was right. So now it's no longer a guess but an established fact. This is crucial information for the consequences are enormous. It means that Dr. Y was certainly in a position to help Gerry and Kate with a place to hide Madeleine's body. In fact a holiday home would be the ideal location; most of the year it's empty and locked up, no callers or postmen or meter readers would even ring the doorbell. I feel that this must be the ideal location to hide something or somebody. Meanwhile my Portuguese contact has sent me an email with the complete address of the property plus a few photographs of the front and back of what I now see is more like a cottage. It's quite small, with a garage at the side and all walls painted white. It has a small patch of greenery at the front and a garden at the back which is rather longer than it is wide. The garden has a small lawn and is planted with some low shrubs. My contact has done sterling work I think, as I pull up Google Maps te see where exactly this doctor's property is located. Would it be near the Ocean Club? Or near the beach? I zoom in on the map and now I have an eagle's eye view of the street where the doctor has his holiday home, very close to the ocean at the edge of the village. I zoom in closer. Do I see that right? I zoom in even more. My heart may well have missed a beat or two; I realize that if this is true, it could change everything. To understand this we have to go back to the statements of the Smith family from Ireland [Chapter The Smiths' Statements]. Three members of the Smith family from Ireland told the police that they saw a man who looked like Gerry, walking with a young blond girl on his arm. And now Google tells me that the location where the Smiths met this man, was no more than twenty paces away from the front door of the cottage belonging to Dr. Y. Can this be true? Was Gerry so close to this cottage? Does this mean that the Smiths did indeed see Gerry carrying Madeleine on his arm? For now we have a location where he may have taken Madeleine. The locked up, empty holiday home belonging to a Portuguese doctor who has many links with the UK and who frequented the same world of medics and academics as the 'Tapas doctors'. And it is exactly here, quite near the front door of the cottage, where the 'man with the child' [i.e. Gerry with Madeleine] is seen by the Smiths. Can this be a coincidence? I hope not, but yes, of course it can. The chance, though, seems small but it is possible. In any case my informant whose full name I don't even know, has given me important information; he has set me on a trail that as far as I know hasn't been followed by anyone concerned in the mystery of the disappearance of Madeleine. As far as I know neither the Polícia Judiciária nor Scotland Yard have followed this up. For both have sidelined the statements from the Smith family and didn't investigate it any further. For no good reason as it now turns out. For now it is possible to confirm the statements of the Smiths with additional information and even with a witness, or is he a suspect? [Dr. Y]. Mainly because we now have a location where Gerry's walk with Madeleine could have terminated. Surely that will be very easy to investigate, certainly for the police. [Note: In my first book about the disappearance, 'The Truth Is Out There', the Smiths' statements are extensively examined and in particular the statement given by Martin Smith. Therefore I am convinced that they, without knowing this for sure at the time, indeed encountered Gerry McCann carrying Madeleine that evening of the disappearance. The time was about 21.45h.] When I have really absorbed all this new information I'm beginning to realize that it will be very difficult to find out if Gerry really was on his way to the holiday home of Dr. Y. The only way to find out if that was indeed the house which was used to hide Madeleine in 2007, is to ask the owner. That's how simple it is; I can't think of any other way. I will phone Dr. Y and ask if it is possible that his house has been used for this purpose, without his knowledge. Maybe he became involved without knowing what the case was? This seems to be the most reasonable option. The doctor deserves the benefit of the doubt.

I decide to put it aside for the moment and work out how to approach the doctor: this needs very careful preparation. I will have to respect whatever he chooses to tell me. For it is by no means certain that he was involved in the disappearance and what's more, he is a doctor, which clearly entitles him to some respect. All I have discovered so far may well be a series of coincidental facts and events, but I still feel that this is a very promising lead. Just to recap: 1] two witnesses note the absence of Gerry in the Tapas bar during a crucial half hour, 2] during that same half hour the Smith family from Ireland see a man who looked like Gerry with a little girl on his arm, 3] who at that time is a few metres away from the front door of the holiday home of Dr. Y. It all seems to fit perfectly, from start to finish and covers all the available evidence for this half hour. And that's not all [...]

For reasons I cannot disclose yet I cannot give further information which I have at my disposal about Dr. Y. Consequently this chapter has been 'redacted' and several details have been removed. If and when circumstances change, I'll publish this information still at a later date.

[Important to know: it is not at all a fact that Dr. Y, who has an excellent reputation, had anything to do with or was involved in the disappearance of Madeleine McCann. But it is necessary, considering the above discussed facts, to establish if his holiday home played a role, possibly without his knowledge, in the disappearance of Madeleine. Although in this book I call Dr. Y. a witness, the police undoubtedly will call him a possible suspect.]

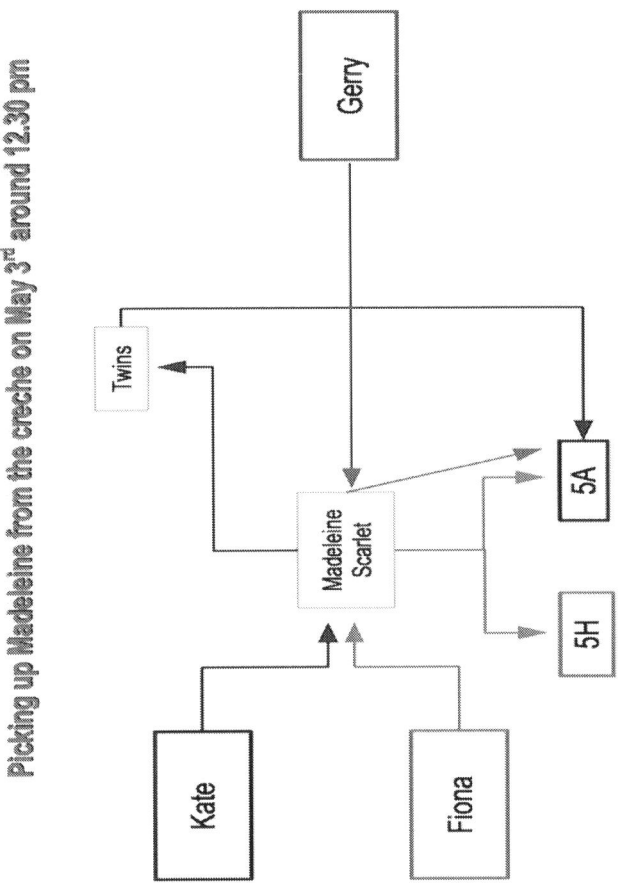

Picking up Madeleine from the creche on May 3rd around 12.30 pm

© Peter Scharrenberg

It is not at all clear who actually picked up Madeleine from the crèche on the day of her disappearance. Three people, three different stories.

26. THE INVISIBLE MEN

As has been discussed in previous chapters it is on the Thursday afternoon that the normal routines of the Tapas group changed dramatically. For a start, the group met around 11.45h at the swimming pool and after that everyone had lunch in their own apartments, whereas before it had been a happy get-together with the adults and the children. Except for the McCanns, who had chosen to have lunch every day in their own apartment. And that is not the only change in the group's routine. Suddenly there is a 'men's social', which means that the men have separate activities, away from their wifes and children. This too, is the first time this happens that week. In fact this meant that David Payne went windsurfing on his own, Russell O'Brien and Matthew Oldfield decided to sail a catamaran and Gerry, with Kate and the children, remained in the apartment after lunch. [Afterwards the McCanns went to the play area and the swimming pool.] What does stand out in this programme is that Gerry didn't take part in the so-called 'men's social'. He stayed with his family that afternoon and didn't go anywhere on his own. At least, that is what he told the police. Now that we know from a previous chapter that it is very unlikely that Russell and Matthew sailed a catamaran that afternoon, the question arises where they all were during that time. In order to answer that question fully it is necessary to take a closer look at the activities of the other men, David Payne and Gerry. What exactly were they doing during that time on the Thursday afternoon? And can we deduce something from their statements? First David Payne. He told the police that he went windsurfing around 13.00h and that he spent most of the afternoon on the board of his windsurfer. It is interesting that he mentions the time he spent windsurfing no less than three times in short succession in his statement, whilst the police only asked him once. Apparently it was important for David Payne to highlight this. Next he stated that when he walked from the Ocean Club to the beach he didn't meet anyone and hadn't taken much notice of people on the beach. Once with his surfboard on the waves he says in his statement that he only saw Russell O'Brien and Matthew Oldfield in the distance, but he didn't see anyone else. It is quite possible, although not entirely credible, that he really didn't see anyone else that Thursday afternoon, but this would mean that no-one else could have seen him either. There are no independent witnesses to affirm that he was indeed surfing, therefore it is not possible to verify David Payne's statement. All one can do is to note his surfing activities as a possible activity, but we cannot take this as an established fact, simply because he said that's what he did. Regrettably after such a long time it isn't possible to find out from the company, which rented out the surfboards, whether David Payne did in fact take a surfboard out that afternoon. The only witnesses who have allegedly seen him riding the waves are Russell O'Brien and Matthew Oldfield, as can be read in their statements to the police. This means that it isn't a hundred percent certain that David Payne was out surfing that afternoon. For neither Russell or Matthew are independent witnesses; they might have had a reason to be economical with the truth. So now we see that David Payne's surfing that afternoon cannot be confirmed, it seems that these three sporting men don't have a solid alibi for that Thursday afternoon. They were 'somewhere on the ocean' and completely out of view. It is indeed as Fiona Payne said in her rogatory interview in 2008: "The men were sort of out of the picture." She hit the nail on the head: the three men were indeed completely 'invisible' that afternoon, which is significant in view of the fact that Madeleine disappeared only hours later. And then we look at Gerry, what did he tell the police at the time about his activities that afternoon? We already know he didn't join the 'men's social' but preferred to stay with Kate and the children. According to his statement he left their apartment after lunch, around 14.00h to take the children with Kate to the play area of the Ocean Club. They stayed there until about 14.30h and took the children to their respective crèches. After this he and Kate went to the tennis courts, where they had a joint tennis lesson from their coach. The lesson ended at 16.30h after which Kate went to the beach to go jogging on her own. It seems a perfectly normal account of the afternoon, and one would not have a problem believing this was the case. However, the problem here is the same as with the three intrepid sailors of the group: not a single independent witness can be found who have seen the McCann family in the play area or on their way to the play area. And that seems very strange; is it true that they themselves didn't see or speak to anyone during that half hour in the play area? Equally strange, nobody else has seen the McCann family there? Not even a member of staff from the Ocean Club? The answer is no. Not one single witness can be found to confirm these statements from Gerry and Kate, not one. In other words: from the moment that they collected the children from the crèche at lunchtime, around 12.30h, nobody saw Gerry until he had a tennis lesson together with Kate at 15.30h. That means that the whereabouts of Gerry [and Kate] cannot be established with any certainty, therefore it is impossible to take the statements from Gerry and Kate on this timespan as a fact. We simply cannot be sure as there is nothing and nobody to confirm these statements. At the same time this means that Gerry is now in the same position as the three sailors, David, Matthew and Russell, who were allegedly 'somewhere on the ocean'. Surely that is strange; four men who suddenly are 'out of sight', haven't been seen by anybody and who themselves haven't seen anybody either. Does this sound at all possible? Three men who walk through the village to the beach, one to go surfing and two to go sailing, and who all like it so much that they're doing this for about three hours, yet never meet a soul. Not on the way there and not whilst they're on the ocean. And the fourth man, Gerry, is in the play area near the swimming pool of the resort, where he doesn't see anybody and he himself hasn't been seen either. Not even when the famous pool photo was taken by Kate. So once again there is no testimony from an independent source to confirm any of these activities and the times they took place. Of course this means that the four men may have been anywhere except it seems, on the ocean. Although Gerry tried to create 'hard' evidence that he was indeed at the swimming pool. For near the end of May he produced a photograph which was made by Kate that Thursday afternoon at 14.29'51h exactly. It is the famous photo of Gerry, Amelie and Madeleine sitting on the edge of the pool of the Ocean Club, enjoying the sun. Unfortunately the anomalies in the swimming pool photo, as analyzed and described in another chapter, were easily spotted and the so-called proof of his presence there at that precise time failed completely. The swimming pool photo is almost certainly a fake. It then follows logically that Gerry and his family apparently weren't in the play area or by the swimming pool, but it appears to have been important for them to make people believe they were there and at that time. Summing up we can say that the four men have no credible alibi as from 12.30h to 15.30h; they could have been anywhere that afternoon. The important questions that arise are: where were they and what were they doing? Because whatever they did it wasn't meant to be disclosed and therefore it is probable that the reason for this secrecy had something to do with Madeleine's disappearance. Otherwise, why would they have given dubious statements about that afternoon and kept their real activities secret? For although there is no hard evidence, it is possible that all four men met in the holiday home of Dr. Y to discuss the situation they found themselves in and to set up the scenario for Madeleine's 'abduction' that evening. [Besides that, somebody had to turn the freezer on so it would be 'ready' later that day.] It is a logical step to assume that David, Russell and Matthew wanted to know what was going on, and of course where, if they were complicit in the coming events. And it seems only logical to assume that they wanted to lend support to their friend and colleague Gerry McCann. The fact that this 'men's social' was invented by the group indicates that the Thursday afternoon was to be a 'men only afternoon'. The men had separated themselves from the rest of the holiday group. Apparently they needed to explain their absence from their families, something that had not happened earlier that week. All that holiday week the men had joined their partners and children for the afternoon, a change in the routine of one or two of the Tapas men would not be that unusual, but all four men of the group disappearing all at the same time stretches credibility too far. In short: the four men in the group were completely out of sight that Thursday afternoon, whilst it is absolutely not clear what they did or where they actually were. Indeed, it is very likely that they invented these alleged activities that afternoon in order to cover up what they were really occupied with that afternoon. As noted earlier, there is no evidence that they did in fact spend the afternoon in the doctor's holiday home to plan the 'abduction'. But neither is there any evidence that they sailed, surfed or were enjoying the sun at the swimming pool that afternoon in Praia da Luz.

27. THE HILL, PART II

It's about 11.00h that morning when I'm driving my rental car towards the praia where I want to go. It isn't a beautiful praia, which is Portuguese for beach, in fact it doesn't look much like a praia. I wonder if I have really interpreted the telephone data correctly and the idea that I might be on my way to the place where Madeleine was buried, sends a cold shiver down my spine. For wouldn't that be amazing? Even so, I'm not going to find out for sure today, I know. Of course I hardly expect a tombstone to mark the grave. But I simply have to go there, for not only will I get to know the area but even more importantly, it will give me a better idea of the lay of the land so to speak, especially the type of soil which would allow one to dig a grave. Certainly, this trip will surely give me a lot more information and I'm so eager to go there, I only notice by the changing note of the engine that I've pushed the rev counter into the red. And there it is at last, the turning for 'my praia'. I switch on the dash-cam so I can have a good look at the route later, and it will also give me the shortest possible time it takes to get from the N125 to the Atlantic Ocean. The route I need to take runs from the N125 south towards the coast. The exit doesn't have a number and I was driving too fast to see if the road had a name. But I don't think so. It's not a very wide road; there is just about enough room for an car coming the other way to pass safely, but you need to keep an eye out for oncoming traffic. I notice that during the first minutes I pass quite a few small buildings. Sheds, walls, stables or barns. Every single one built on the slope of a hill. After about one minute in this area I'm still driving towards the ocean. And the the view changes dramatically. A lot of green to the left and right, but nowhere where you could park your car without blocking the road in some way. After about five minutes driving the meandering road straightens out, I can't yet see the ocean, but I do see a wide open plain in front of me. Following the road which should bring me closer to the praia takes me, after a few hundred metres, to a large carpark. I estimate that there is enough room for at least thirty cars. [But I know that this carpark wasn't there in 2007.] I get out of the car, grab my cameras and start to take some pictures. A little further on I can see the whole point of this journey in all its glory: the remains of an old fort that looks like a small house, without a roof. And in fact the walls aren't looking too good either. Not exactly something to get enthusiastic about. But it certainly confirms my feeling that there is simply nothing to do here. The beach, a small strip of sand, isn't worth the journey either. It beats me how anyone would want to stay here for more than ten minutes, there's nothing to do, nowhere to enjoy a meal or a drink. Basically most people happening on this spot would leave it to go to one of the pleasant and accessible coastal villages. I simply can't imagine that the McCanns were so taken by this spot that they visited it five times in seven days. To do what? There is simply nothing to see or do here. Five times in seven days? I start to walk up the hill, it isn't very hard for the incline is relatively low so the climb won't exhaust me. I note that I've taken less than ten minutes to reach the top. Turning around I see the large carpark down in the lee of the hill. I note that it is hardly possible to see my car from this distance, useful to know I think. I walk on, further up the hill, until I reach the summit, you could say the cliff edge of the hill. Now I can see and hear the ocean driving the waves against the solid rocks below; if I stumble or fall here, it will be the end of me for sure. Now I have seen the area I need to take some soil samples. I need to know where it is possible to dig down to 'any' depth on this hill. Everywhere around me are bushes, high and low and groundcover by what looks like a sort of heather. But I can also see quite a few areas of 'bare' soil, that is to say, rocky surfaces and very hard compacted soil. So I'm testing the soil, digging with my bare hands to determine how hard it really is. Then I break off a branch from a large bush and use it to scratch the ground; I notice that there are lots of places were the ground is loose enough to dig a hole. This is not the case everywhere, the ground of some areas is simply too rocky to dig in, so I can forget those places. At one point I look down the slope of the hill and notice that the carpark has disappeared from sight, I can't see it from where I am now. Here I look at the ground and note that one could indeed dig a hole here, the soil is loose enough to do so. Not only that, but you're also completely out of sight of the carpark and the surrounding area, as I now discover. Yes, this would be an excellent place to secretly bury someone, that seems clear to me. Any hikers can be seen in the far distance long before they'd get anywhere near this spot, and besides that, I can't imagine why a hiker would choose to climb this particular hill. I haven't seen anyone all these hours I've been here. It strengthens my feeling that Madeleine could very well have been buried here. A lot of privacy, light dry soil which is easy to dig and lots of places where it is possible to do so without anyone seeing you. And then the car, parked neatly out of sight on, of all places, a convenient and discretely hidden carpark. Who would find that suspicious? No, it's getting more and more obvious to me, this would have been a safe place for the McCanns to bury Madeleine. Taking into account all the pings, statements and other matters, it seems to me to be a logical location for Gerry and Kate to do so. I sit down on the ground and take my time to look around. Could Madeleine be buried around here? Did Gerry and Kate walk around this area on the evening of the 1st of August 2007, in total darkness? With their dead little daughter wrapped in her pink princess blanket and in Gerry's large sports bag? For the Polícia Judiciária later found these items [recorded in the early photographs of the apartment] were missing. It is very likely that the blanket and the sportsbag were buried with her; for I cannot imagine that they would simply have put Madeleine in a makeshift grave without any protection or anything to cover her. And then just covered her body with sand and earth to close the grave. After another long 360° look around I get up, I've seen enough, it is definitely possible to use this rugged hill for a primitive, 'secret funeral'. That in any case is my conclusion as I walk back to my car. This area should be searched by the Polícia Judiciária and their cadaver dogs; surely there are now more than enough reasons to do so. I suddenly realize that this hill is the first location which can logically be argued to be Madeleine's last resting place, for the arguments are solidly based on telephone pings, dates, various statements, frequency of visits to the area and the suitability of the terrain. Forensic investigations by the Polícia Judiciária using cadaver dogs around the apartment, amongst other locations frequented by the McCanns, may more or less have been meant to exclude certain areas; the police would not have any reason to believe why she would be buried there. I have a last look at the carpark in my rear view mirror as I drive off. Yes, this could really be it, the place, the location, the hill, the desolate hill that haunted Kate so much. Far away from any habitation, with a lot of privacy and an ideal site to park a car. What else would they have needed? I drive back to my hotel for I need time to evaluate this new information and to decide what my next step has to be. I toy with the notion of informing the Polícia Judiciária in Porto of my discoveries. [The investigative team moved from Portimão to Porto, some 400 miles north of Praia da Luz.] Perhaps I'll be able to convince them to search this hill with a team of cadaver dogs. And of course, should they do so, I'd want to be there. Getting to the junction I turn right to get back onto the N125, in the direction of Praia da Luz. It's been a good day for my investigation and I decide to spend the evening analyzing all the information I've gathered. It's my last evening in Portugal, I'm flying back to Amsterdam tomorrow, where I will continue my research with these new facts that have come to light. But I know that it won't be long before I return to the small coastal village in the Algarve. As I drive to my hotel I think of Madeleine, she would have been sixteen years old now. She would have had a life of her own, with friends, classmates and maybe even a boyfriend. But all that was not destined for her. Those thoughts make me sad, to be honest. But it also motivates me to continue my work on this case, for I have only one thing on my mind: her disappearance cannot go unsolved, it just can't. Madeleine deserves justice. Period.

Some of my readers will no doubt wonder why I haven't made the results of my investigation available to the Portuguese police. I can tell them that I have in fact done so. On Wednesday the **24th April** last, just before this book was published, I had a pleasant 40 minute telephone conversation with Dr. Helena Monteiro, who is the lead investigator in this case in Portugal. I presented her several new clues and even the name of a completely new suspect, [Dr. Y.] as well as the possible 'safe house' that was used to hide Madeleine. She assured me that she would study the information I gave her and that she would compare it with some undisclosed information presently available to her. However, she did tell me that a scenario which includes the parents as being involved in the disappearance is no longer considered a possibility. But she added that 'everything is possible'.

Nine days later, on **May 3rd,** the leading Portuguese news outlet 'Correia da Manhã' reported that just last month the PJ had 'suddenly' received new information in the case that was considered as credible by the investigators. The Prosecutor stated that there were 'strong new clues' which investigators have to follow up. They even had a new suspect in sight. According to 'CdM' the investigation team was extended with more Inspectors and was awarded with more funding.

Many thanks to all who helped and supported me writing this book, in particular my good friend Paul G. and Patrice B., my tireless guide in Portugal. Special thanks to my translator for her excellent work. My very special thanks to an old friend for his very big help with my research. Muito obrigado! And last but certainly not least, I also want to thank all the readers of my first book about the disappearance. Thank you for all the comments and feedback.

Sources consulted for this book:

Polícia Judiciária-dossier, New Scotland Yard, Madeleine McCann Foundation, Madeleine Fund, 'The Truth of the Lie' /Gonçalo Amaral, McCannfiles.com, McCannPJfiles, BBC, 'Faked Abduction' /Brian Johnson, 'Madeleine' /Kate McCann, TheMaddieCaseFiles, FindMadeleine.com, gerrymccannsblogs.co.uk., Dr. Martin Roberts, several survival experts, Signi Search Dogs, The Countrywide Unit of the Dutch National Police, Adela Morris of the Institute of Canine Forensics, California, USA, Institute of Legal Medicine, University Medical Center Hamburg, Germany, Center Forensic Imaging and Virtopsy of the University of Bern, Switserland, State Police Academy [LPS36], Department of the Interior, Hamburg, Germany and the Police Faculty, Technical College for Public Administration, Hamburg, Germany.

Printed in Great Britain
by Amazon

49962267R00106